D0589555

the **official** guide to
LEARNING
TO DRIVE

London: TSO

Written and compiled by Driving Standards Agency (DSA) Publications.

Published with the permission of the Driving Standards Agency on behalf of the Controller of Her Majesty's Stationery Office.

© Crown Copyright 2004.

All rights reserved. Applications for reproduction should be made in writing to Commercial Department, Driving Standards Agency, Stanley House, 56 Talbot Street, Nottingham, NG1 5GU.

Previously known as *Your Driving Test*
First edition 1990
Second edition 1993

The Official Driving Test
Third edition 1996
Fourth edition 1999
Fifth edition 2001
Sixth edition 2003

New title - *The Official DSA Guide to Learning to Drive*
Seventh edition 2004

ISBN 0 11 552608 0

A CIP catalogue record for this book is available from the British Library.

Other titles in the Driving series

The Official Theory Test for Car Drivers
The Official Theory Test for Motorcyclists
The Official Theory Test for Drivers of Large Vehicles
Driving - the essential skills
The Official Guide to Accompanying Learner Drivers
Motorcycle Riding – the essential skills
Official Motorcycling – CBT and practical test
Driving Buses and Coaches – the official DSA syllabus
Driving Goods Vehicles – the official DSA syllabus
The Official Guide to Tractor and Specialist Vehicle Driving Tests
The Official Theory Test CDrom – for car drivers
The Official Theory Test CDrom – for motorcyclists
The Official Guide to Hazard Perception DVD
Roadsense – the official guide to hazard perception VHS
The Official Guide to Learning to Drive DVD

Acknowledgements

The Driving Standards Agency would like to thank their staff and the Department for Transport for their contribution to the production of this publication:

We would also like to thank Thule for supplying photographs for the loading section.

Every effort has been made to ensure that the information contained in this publication is accurate at the time of going to press. The Stationery Office cannot be held responsible for any inaccuracies. Information in this book is for guidance only.

All metric and imperial conversions in this book are approximate.

Theory and practical tests

(Bookings and enquiries)

DSA 0870 01 01 372
Fax 0870 01 04 372
Minicom 0870 01 06 372
Welsh speakers 0870 01 00 372

DVTA (Northern Ireland)
Theory test 0845 600 6700
Practical test 0870 247 2472

Driving Standards Agency

(Headquarters)

Stanley House, 56 Talbot Street,
Nottingham NG1 5GU

Tel 0115 901 2500
Fax 0115 901 2510

Driver and Vehicle Testing Agency

(Headquarters)

Balmoral Road, Belfast BT12 6QL

Tel 02890 681831
Fax 02890 665520

Driver Vehicle Licensing Agency

(GB Licence Enquiries)

Tel 0870 240 0009
Fax 01792 783071
Minicom 01792 782787

Driver and Vehicle Licensing

(Northern Ireland)

Tel 02870 341469
24 hour tel 0345 111 222
Minicom 02870 341 380

Mobility Advice and Vehicle Information Service (MAVIS)

'O' Wing, MacAdam Avenue,
Old Wokingham Road, Crowthorne
Berkshire RG45 6XD

Tel 01344 661000
Fax 01344 661066

Office of the Parliamentary Commissioner for Administration

(The Parliamentary Ombudsman)

Millbank Tower, Millbank, London
SW1P 4QP

Tel 020 7217 4163
Fax 020 7217 4160

The Driving Standards Agency (DSA) is an executive agency of the Department for Transport. You'll see its logo at test centres.

DSA aims to promote road safety through the advancement of driving standards, by

- establishing and developing high standards and best practice in driving and riding on the road; before people start to drive, as they learn, and after they pass their test
- ensuring high standards of instruction for different types of driver and rider
- conducting the statutory theory and practical tests efficiently, fairly and consistently across the country
- providing a centre of excellence for driver training and driving standards
- developing a range of publications and other publicity material designed to promote safe driving for life.

www.dsa.gov.uk

The Driver and Vehicle Testing Agency (DVTA) is an executive agency within the Department of the Environment for Northern Ireland.

Its primary aim is to promote and improve road safety through the advancement of driving standards and implementation of the Government's policies for improving the mechanical standards of vehicles.

www.doeni.gov.uk/dvta

CONTENTS

section **one**

SAFETY AND YOUR VEHICLE

This section covers

- before you start
- structured learning
- your instructor
- practising
- notes for the accompanying driver
- official study aids

A message from the Chief Driving Examiner

Being able to drive on your own gives you a whole new world of independence. It's important that when you get to the stage of taking your practical test you are not only ready to pass, but are prepared for a lifetime of safe driving.

In this book we show the Key Skills you need to learn before taking your test. We refer to the *Driver's Record*, if you don't have one of these, ask your instructor for one, or you can download one from www.dsa.gov.uk

You need to be capable of driving consistently, without prompting, to **Level 5** in the *Driver's Record* before you take your practical test. Most people fail their test because they're not fully prepared, so make sure you have covered all the Key Skills to the standard we show in this book.

The key to gaining these skills is good tuition and plenty of practice.

Robin Cummins
The Chief Driving Examiner
Driving Standards Agency

Before you start

First things first

You have decided you want to learn to drive. This will give you the opportunity to learn a completely new skill, one that will open up a whole new world of independence. But driving also comes with responsibility - it's important that you know how to drive safely and responsibly, that you learn the skills and practise so you become a safe driver, not just to pass the test but for life.

The first step is getting a provisional driving licence, but even before that you have to know that your eyesight is good enough to drive on the road.

Your eyesight

You can't drive on the road unless your eyesight meets certain requirements.

The easiest way to check this yourself is to try to read a number plate at the specified distance and if you can't, you should visit an optician before you start to drive.

The regulations state that, in good daylight, you should be able to read a vehicle number plate with letters 79.4 mm (3.1 in.) high at a minimum distance of 20.5 metres (about 67 feet). These are normally the number plates in the older format (for example X123XXX).

Number plates in the format (XX50XXX) have a narrower font and should be read from a distance of 20 metres (66 feet).

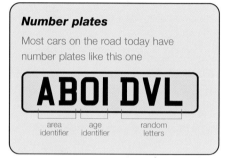

Number plates

Most cars on the road today have number plates like this one

ABO1 DVL

area identifier | age identifier | random letters

If you need glasses or contact lenses to read the number plate, that's fine. However, you must wear them whenever you drive. If you have had sight correction surgery you should declare this when you apply for your provisional licence.

You are responsible for ensuring that your eyesight meets the minimum legal requirements every time you drive. The police can stop you at any time and ask you to take an eyesight test. You'll also have to take one at the start of your practical test.

Applying for your licence

You must be at least 17 years old before you can get a provisional car licence. However, as an exception, if you receive Disability Living Allowance at the higher rate, you can get your provisional licence when you're 16.

Remember, you must have received your provisional driving licence before you start to drive on the road - this means that you must actually have it in your possession, not just have sent away for it.

Driving licences are issued by the Driver and Vehicle Licensing Agency (DVLA) and you can get an application form (D1) from any Post Office. In Northern Ireland the issuing authority is Driver and Vehicle Licensing Northern Ireland and the form is a DL1.

Send your completed form to the appropriate office (details are given on the form). Remember to include a passport-type photograph as all provisional licences now issued are photocard licences.

When you receive your provisional licence, check that all the details are correct. If you need to contact DVLA or DVLNI, telephone numbers are shown on p3.

Structured learning

Those who pass their driving test have had, *on average*, about 45 hours of professional training combined with 22 hours of private practice.

Learners who prepare this way, with a combination of plenty of professional training and plenty of practice, do better on test.

To help you learn in a structured way, DSA has produced a *Driver's Record*.

The Driver's Record

The *Driver's Record* is a way of helping you and your driving instructor (see p12) keep a record of your progress while you're learning to drive. You may have received one with your provisional licence.

Following a structured learning programme, such as that contained in the driver's record, is beneficial to both you as a learner and your instructor. You need to learn the skill and then practise to get the experience.

You also need to learn both the theory and practical driving at the same time, especially now that the theory test contains a hazard perception part.

The record is a pocket-sized leaflet that you should take with you to all your driving lessons.

The *Driver's Record* contains a list of all the Key Skills which you need to achieve in order to pass your test and become a safe driver. It has space for your instructor to fill in as you progress through the various levels shown on the Record.

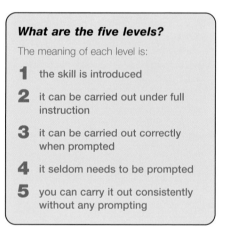

What are the five levels?

The meaning of each level is:

1 the skill is introduced

2 it can be carried out under full instruction

3 it can be carried out correctly when prompted

4 it seldom needs to be prompted

5 you can carry it out consistently without any prompting

Levels 1 to 4 should be initialled and dated by your instructor, and full details added when you reach **Level 5**. From this, you and your instructor will be able to see at a glance which topics you need to improve. Details of the 24 Key Skills can be found on p18-67 of this book.

An important part of the structured learning process is practising what you have learnt during your lessons. Get together with your instructor and the person who will be helping you to practise and discuss what you need to practise.

You can keep a record of any practice you have on different types of road and during different conditions between lessons on p98-101. Fill these in when you go out with the person helping you to practise. You can also record any worries you may have about your driving and then discuss these with your instructor (alternatively, printed sheets are available from your instructor).

You aren't ready to take your test until you have a complete set of signatures in the **Level 5** boxes. Only then can your instructor sign the declaration.

Where can I get hold of a Driver's Record?

If you haven't got one, ask your instructor, get one from your local driving test centre or download one from **www.dsa.gov.uk**

By this time you should be able to drive safely without prompting from your instructor or the person helping you to practise. Don't forget to take the Record with you when you go for your practical driving test.

Keep this as a record of your 'Learning to Drive' experience.

The Driver's Record will help to remind you what you're trying to achieve, how to get there and how far you've got

Your instructor

If you're going to pay someone to teach you to drive, they must be an Approved Driving Instructor (ADI) or hold a trainee licence.

DSA is responsible for checking the instructional standards of ADIs. All ADIs must

- have held a full driving licence for at least four years
- pass a challenging theory and practical test
- reach and keep up a high standard of instruction. ADIs are regularly checked by a DSA supervising examiner
- be registered with DSA
- display a green ADI identification certificate on the windscreen of the tuition vehicle during lessons.

It's unlikely that anyone except an ADI would have the experience, knowledge and training to teach you properly.

Some trainee driving instructors are granted a trainee licence so that they can gain teaching experience before their qualifying examination. This licence is a pink identification certificate which must be displayed on the windscreen of the tuition vehicle during lessons.

Choosing an ADI

Ask friends and relatives for recommendations. Choose an instructor who has a good reputation, is reliable and punctual and whose car suits you. Ask the instructor for their grade before starting a course of lessons.

What does each instructor grade mean?

The standard of instruction of all ADIs is regularly checked by DSA. The instructor is then given a grade.

4 is satisfactory

5 is a good overall standard

6 is the highest

Remember, you can always ask to see the instructor's grade report.

Choosing the right instructor is vital to helping you develop as a driver. A good instructor will be happy to answer all your questions

Ask if they have signed up to the industry Code of Practice. This is a voluntary code which covers the following

- their level of qualification
- the personal conduct expected from them when giving tuition
- the professional conduct of their business
- the acceptability of their advertising
- their method of dealing with complaints.

For further information or advice telephone DSA on 0115 901 2500.

Take advice from your ADI - your instructor will be able to help with all aspects of driving and advise you on

- what to study - DSA produce a range of books, CD-Roms and DVDs to help you learn to drive
- how to practise and what you should be practising
- when you are ready for your test
- further training after you've passed your test (*Pass Plus* scheme see p80).

What if I find don't like my instructor after I start lessons?

You can always find yourself a new instructor. It's important that you get on well with whoever is teaching you to drive. Different people prefer different teaching styles. You should try to find someone that suits you.

Can I have lessons in my own car?

Some instructors are prepared to give lessons in your own car, if you are lucky enough to have a car. Ask about this when you first contact them as some instructors will not do so for health and safety reasons.

Practising

As stated earlier, those who pass their driving test have had, on average, about 45 hours of professional training combined with 22 hours of private practice. This is the average, but generally the more driving experience you get the better.

You need to gain experience on all different types of road and driving conditions. The more you practise and increase your experience, the more confident you will become.

Your accompanying driver

The person helping you to practise must be at least 21 years old and hold a full driving licence for the category of vehicle being driven (they must have held this for at least the last three years).

The practice vehicle

The vehicle in which you practise must be roadworthy and properly insured for you to drive. If you drive while uninsured you will be committing a serious offence. The vehicle must also display L plates to the front and rear - make sure they are secure and don't obstruct your view.

Get together with both your instructor and the person who will be helping you to practise so you can discuss what you need to do. Ask your instructor for advice on what skills you should practise after each lesson.

How to practise

You should vary what you do. Try to practise

- on as many types of road as you can
- in all sorts of traffic and weather conditions, even in the dark
- on dual carriageways where the national speed limit applies. You may be asked to drive on this type of road during the test.

As you practise in these different conditions and different types of road, log your hours and miles on p98-101. This will help you to remember and quantify the amount of practice you have had in the different conditions.

When you practise, try to

- avoid obstructing other traffic. Most drivers are tolerant of learners, but don't try their patience too much
- consider the local residents. For example, don't repeatedly practise emergency stops in the same quiet residential streets or practise on test routes
- get lots of general driving. Don't just concentrate on the exercises included in the practical test.

There are more helpful suggestions for the person accompanying you in the official DSA book *Helping Learners to Practise*.

Notes for the accompanying driver

Agreeing to accompany a learner is a responsibility not to be taken lightly. You will be the person helping your learner get that important extra practice.

Your help won't replace good professional tuition but it will enable your learner to get the experience while driving in different conditions

You must make sure that you have the right licence and that your car is insured for them to drive (see previous page). You will also need L plates and an additional interior mirror so that you can check what's happening behind.

When you accompany a learner you're responsible for their actions. You'll need to stay calm and offer advice when needed.

Have a chat with your learner and their instructor so that together you can decide what needs to be practised.

Record your time spent in different situations on p98-101. This gives a permanent record of time spent and miles travelled and will help the three of you work out where extra practice would be useful.

Everyone learns at a different pace and finds different things difficult. Something that you find easy may be difficult for a learner. Be patient and constructive. Make sure you're aware of the standard that is expected of a learner driver and the style of driving they are being taught. Some things may have changed since you learnt to drive and it can be confusing for the learner to receive different messages.

> **Remember,** you can't receive payment for the time you spend helping your learner to practise.

There's lots of useful information and loads of hints and tips in the DSA book *Helping Learners to Practise.*

Official study aids

Lessons and practice are the most important elements of learning to drive, but there is something you can do when you're not in the car. There are various books and electronic products to help you with all stages of driving - theory, hazard perception and practical.

The Highway Code - contains all the up to date rules and regulations about using the roads. It's essential reading for everyone - buy a copy of the latest edition, it will be a most useful reference book.

DSA also produce a series of books and electronic products to provide you with a sound knowledge of driving skills.

The Official Theory Test for Car Drivers - includes all the questions and answers in the multiple choice part of the theory test and it explains why all the answers are correct - lots of useful information. It now also includes *The Highway Code*. The questions are regularly updated, make sure that you have the latest version. If you're well prepared you won't find the questions difficult.

This information is also produced in CD-Rom format for those who prefer an interactive way of learning. In this format you can take as many mock tests as you like before you actually take your test for real.

The Official Guide to Hazard Perception - is an interactive DVD to help you prepare for the hazard perception parts of the theory and practical tests.

These training materials are available by mail order from **0870 241 4523**. They are also available from all good bookshops and other outlets.

Or buy online at **www.dsa.gov.uk**

It has clear guidance on how to recognise and respond to hazards and is packed with useful tips, quizzes and expert advice. It includes official hazard perception video clips with feedback on your performance. *Roadsense* is a video and workbook based programme containing much the same information.

The CD-Rom and DVD are available individually or packaged together as *The Official Theory Test Kit* which provides all the learning materials for the theory test in one package.

Driving - the essential skills - the Key Skills section of this book has references to *Driving - the essential skills*. It contains a wealth of information about driving skills, from the very basic, helping you when you first start to drive, through to in-depth advice about dealing with various road and traffic conditions.

The Learning to Drive DVD - has been produced alongside this book. It's presented in a very lively and animated way. It shows the standard at which you need to drive to reach

Level 5 in the *Driver's Record*. This interactive DVD helps you to understand what is needed to reach the standard and gives you many hints and tips to becoming a safe driver. It also shows how the examiner conducts the practical driving test taking you through various parts of the test with the young presenter.

Helping Learners to Practise - the driver who accompanies you will find this book invaluable.

section **two**
KEY SKILLS

This section covers

- legal responsibilities
- cockpit checks
- safety checks
- controls and instruments
- moving away and stopping
- safe positioning
- mirrors - vision and use
- signals
- anticipation and planning
- use of speed
- other traffic
- junctions
- roundabouts
- pedestrian crossings
- dual carriageways
- turning the vehicle around
- reversing
- parking
- emergency stop
- darkness
- weather conditions
- environmental issues
- carrying passengers and loads
- security

Using this book

Use this book as a reference while you are learning to drive.
It can also be used to keep a record of your progress

Reaching Level 5

All the Key Skills from the *Driver's Record* are shown on the following pages. On these pages you'll find details about what standard you need to reach to become a safe driver in that skill and achieve a **Level 5** marking in your *Driver's Record*.

As your instructor signs off the skill in your *Driver's Record*, make a note on the relevant page in this book.

Expert tips

As well as explaining the level that you need to achieve, there are also useful tips from the people who set the tests. These have been drawn up from years of experience and from common mistakes made by candidates during their driving tests.

Further information about the skills can also be found under the references listed at the foot of the page, these are references to *The Highway Code* and *Driving - the essential skills*.

Recap questions

For each skill there are recap questions - try answering these to refresh your memory.

All the answers to the recap questions can be found in the books referred to at the foot of the page.

What to expect on test

Once you have reached **Level 5** in all the key skills and are ready to take your test, there's some useful information about what to expect on the test and what the examiner will be looking for when you're taking it.

Legal responsibilities

As a driver it is your responsibility to know how the law relates to both yourself and your vehicle, so make sure you're up-to-date with the rules and regulations

You need to comply with the **rules and regulations**:

LEVEL 5 — You are in a fit condition to drive safely

To do this you need to understand how the following affects you...

- **health** - certain medical conditions must be reported to DVLA

- **eyesight** - can you read a number plate as shown on p8. If you need glasses to read it clearly then you must always wear them when you're driving

- **drink** - don't drink and drive, there's a legal limit but it's safer not to drink at all if you're going to drive

- **drugs** - never take illegal drugs before driving, the effect can be more severe than alcohol, and even some prescription drugs can make you drowsy

- **tiredness** - if you're tired you're more likely to have an accident. On a long journey have a break every two hours or so

- **mobile phones** - it's illegal to use a hand held phone while driving and even hands free can distract you from your driving.

LEVEL 5 — You and the car you're driving comply with the regulations

To do this you must ensure that...

- the vehicle is taxed and has a valid MOT certificate if it's more than three years old

- the vehicle is insured for you to drive

- the vehicle is in a roadworthy condition

- your driving licence is in order.

L plates should *be clearly displayed on the front and back of the vehicle you're driving (D plates can be used in Wales)*

Remember, you need to know the traffic rules and regulations - these can be found in *The Highway Code* - make sure you know the regulations, ignorance is no defence.

What's the eyesight test?

You have to take an eyesight test before you start your practical test. Details of the requirements are given on p8.

Who can teach me to drive?

Only ADIs and trainee licence holders can teach for payment. They must display a badge on the windscreen during lessons.

Tips from the experts

Make sure you know what to do if you have an accident. Keep calm and as well as dealing with the scene of the accident you may need to report it to the police.

Even hands-free phones distract you from your driving so it's safer not to use one at all. Switch your phone off otherwise you might be tempted to answer it if it rings. Stop safely to retrieve any messages.

The regulations about mobile phones also apply to the person accompanying you as you practise.

What to expect on test

You'll be asked questions about documents during your theory test. You'll need to show the relevant papers and pass the eyesight check before starting your practical test.

Keep a record

Your instructor should keep a record of your progress on your *Driver's Record*. You may also like to fill in your progress below and make any notes that might help you, in this space:

1	3	5
introduced	prompted	independant

Notes

References   **The Highway Code** most of the Code   **Driving** section 2

Cockpit checks

These checks may be simple, but they are essential. The car you are using needs to be comfortable and ready for you to drive before you turn the key in the ignition

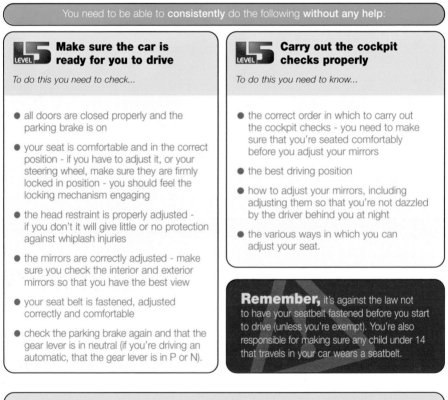

You need to be able to **consistently** do the following **without any help**:

LEVEL 5 — Make sure the car is ready for you to drive

To do this you need to check...

- all doors are closed properly and the parking brake is on

- your seat is comfortable and in the correct position - if you have to adjust it, or your steering wheel, make sure they are firmly locked in position - you should feel the locking mechanism engaging

- the head restraint is properly adjusted - if you don't it will give little or no protection against whiplash injuries

- the mirrors are correctly adjusted - make sure you check the interior and exterior mirrors so that you have the best view

- your seat belt is fastened, adjusted correctly and comfortable

- check the parking brake again and that the gear lever is in neutral (if you're driving an automatic, that the gear lever is in P or N).

LEVEL 5 — Carry out the cockpit checks properly

To do this you need to know...

- the correct order in which to carry out the cockpit checks - you need to make sure that you're seated comfortably before you adjust your mirrors

- the best driving position

- how to adjust your mirrors, including adjusting them so that you're not dazzled by the driver behind you at night

- the various ways in which you can adjust your seat.

Remember, it's against the law not to have your seatbelt fastened before you start to drive (unless you're exempt). You're also responsible for making sure any child under 14 that travels in your car wears a seatbelt.

Can I adjust the mirrors while I'm driving?

Never try to do this on the move - if you need to readjust your mirrors or seat position, find a safe place to stop first.

Do I need to do these checks every time?

Get into the habit of doing these checks every time - it's particularly important if other people use the car.

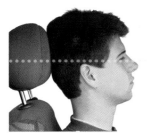
The rigid part of the restraint should support the back of your head

Fasten your seatbelt every time, its against the law not to do so

Make sure the gear lever is in neutral before starting the engine

Tips from the experts

Make sure you do these checks, in the right order, before you start the engine. This is particularly important if you are not the only person using the car.

What to expect on test

Your examiner will watch to make sure that you carry out all the checks, in the right order, before you start the engine.

Recap questions

Q1 Is it the responsibility of the driver to make sure that adult passengers wear seatbelts?

Q2 What could be a consequence of failing to carry out the cockpit checks properly?

Q3 Why should you check that the head restraint is in the correct position?

Keep a record   Notes

Your instructor should keep a record of your progress on your *Driver's Record*. You may also like to fill in your progress below and make any notes that might help you, in this space:

1 introduced

2 full instruction

3 prompted

4 seldom prompted

5 independant

References   **The Highway Code** rule 73 & 75   **Driving** sections 3-5

Safety checks

It's important that your car is in good working order before you start the engine. You need to be aware of what you need to check, how to do it and how often to do it

You need to be able to **consistently** do the following **without any help**:

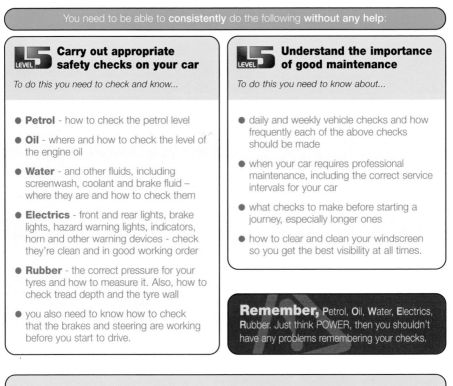

LEVEL 5 — Carry out appropriate safety checks on your car

To do this you need to check and know...

- **Petrol** - how to check the petrol level
- **Oil** - where and how to check the level of the engine oil
- **Water** - and other fluids, including screenwash, coolant and brake fluid – where they are and how to check them
- **Electrics** - front and rear lights, brake lights, hazard warning lights, indicators, horn and other warning devices - check they're clean and in good working order
- **Rubber** - the correct pressure for your tyres and how to measure it. Also, how to check tread depth and the tyre wall
- you also need to know how to check that the brakes and steering are working before you start to drive.

LEVEL 5 — Understand the importance of good maintenance

To do this you need to know about...

- daily and weekly vehicle checks and how frequently each of the above checks should be made
- when your car requires professional maintenance, including the correct service intervals for your car
- what checks to make before starting a journey, especially longer ones
- how to clear and clean your windscreen so you get the best visibility at all times.

Remember, Petrol, Oil, Water, Electrics, Rubber. Just think POWER, then you shouldn't have any problems remembering your checks.

Can I check all this myself?

You'll need to get someone to help you check the brake lights. It's also easier and quicker to check the other lights if you can get someone to look while you are working the controls.

What kind of questions will I be asked on test?

There is only a limited number of safety check questions that you can be asked on test. They can all be found on our website **www.dsa.gov.uk**

Tips from the experts

Make sure that you're familiar with the car you're driving, and that you can explain or demonstrate how you would carry out simple safety checks on that car.

You will need to open the bonnet to carry out some of the checks - make sure you know how to open the bonnet and also that you shut it properly once you've carried out the checks.

Regular servicing will keep the engine more efficient and save you money in the long run.

What to expect on test

At the start of the test your examiner will ask you one of each of the following

- to explain how you would carry out certain safety checks
- to demonstrate how you would carry out certain safety checks.

Recap question

Q1 *What's the minimum tread depth for your car tyres?*

Keep a record

Your instructor should keep a record of your progress on your *Driver's Record*. You may also like to fill in your progress below and make any notes that might help you, in this space:

1 introduced

2 full instruction

3 prompted

4 seldom prompted

5 independant

Notes

References   The Highway Code rules 72-73 & annex 6   **Driving** sections 5 & 14

Controls and instruments

You need to concentrate on what's happening around you when you're driving, so operating the vehicle's controls should be second nature

You need to be able to **consistently** do the following **without any help:**

LEVEL 5 Operate the controls safely without looking

To do this you need to be able to correctly use the...

- **foot controls** - the accelerator, clutch and footbrake pedals

- **hand controls** - the parking brake, steering wheel, indicators, headlights and gearstick

- **other controls** - the horn (you need to know when and for what reason you can legally use the horn), windscreen wipers, demister and heated windows. You also need to be aware of any controls specific to the car you are driving.

Remember, you need to be aware of the consequences of what happens if you use the controls incorrectly.

LEVEL 5 Read the various instruments of the car you're driving

To do this you need to know...

- the meaning and function of each element of the instrument panel including the warning lights and speedometer.

Your speedometer must show miles per hour and kilometres per hour

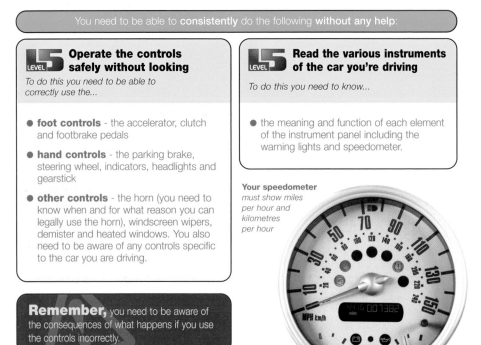

Can I look at the gear lever?

If the car is moving you shouldn't take your eyes off the road to look at the gear lever. You should already know what gear you're in. Don't coast with the gear lever in neutral or the clutch pedal down.

Should I steer and change gear at the same time?

You need both hands to steer. Try to change to the appropriate gear and then put both hands back on the wheel before starting to turn the steering wheel.

Tips from the experts

Balance your use of the accelerator and clutch so that you pull away smoothly and then accelerate gradually to gain speed. Don't accelerate fiercely or use the clutch sharply.

If you're driving an automatic car, make sure you understand the procedure fully.

Brake smoothly and in good time and don't apply the parking brake until the car has stopped. Make sure you don't try to move off with the parking brake on.

Choose the right gear for your speed and the road conditions and ensure that you're in the correct gear to deal with any hazard or junction safely.

Check the correct position for your hands on the steering wheel, keep your steering steady and smooth.

What to expect on test

Your examiner will want to see that you can

● demonstrate good control of the vehicle throughout the test

● show an understanding of the vehicle's instruments.

Recap question

Q1 *When is it illegal to use your horn?*

Keep a record

Notes

Your instructor should keep a record of your progress on your *Driver's Record*. You may also like to fill in your progress below and make any notes that might help you, in this space:

1 introduced	**3** prompted	**5**
2 full instruction	**4** seldom prompted	independant

References The Highway Code rules 73, 90-102 Driving section 3

Moving away and stopping

You have to do these every time you drive, that's why it's so important to make sure that you know the correct procedures for moving away and stopping safely

You need to be able to **consistently** do the following **without any help**:

Move away and stop again safely

To do this you need to...

- be able to carry out both manoeuvres on level ground, on a hill, at an angle and straight ahead

- use the MSM and PSL routines

- observe what is happening around you and be aware of any blind spots

- co-ordinate your use of the accelerator, clutch and footbrake so that you move off and slow down safely and smoothly

- be able to use the parking brake and steering competently

- know where and when to look, what to look for and how to act safely on what you see

- be able to identify suitable stopping places

- know where and when to signal.

Remember, the MSM and PSL routines are key to virtually all aspects of driving

Mirrors - Signal - Manoeuvre

M use your mirrors to check the position of traffic around and behind you

S show others what you intend to do. Always signal in good time

M a change in speed or position - slowing down, stopping, turning...

Position - Speed - Look

P position your car correctly for the move you want to make

S adjust your speed so it is appropriate for the manoeuvre

L have a final look to check it's safe before you start to steer.

What if I don't have a clear view of the road?

If you can't see because someone has parked close to you, edge out slowly and only move off when you can see it's safe.

How do I stop if someone is following very closely?

Make sure you signal in good time to let them know that you're going to slow down and stop.

You may need to check your blind spot more than once when moving off from behind another car

Tips from the experts

Always use your mirrors but only signal if you need to, don't just signal automatically.

Check your blind spots. Don't pull out without looking or make anyone else stop or swerve.

Move off smoothly in the correct gear and don't accelerate excessively.

What to expect on test

Your examiner may ask you to stop at the side of the road and then move away again. Every time you perform either of these manoeuvres the examiner will watch your

- use of the controls and MSM routine each time you move off and stop - don't forget to incorporate the PSL routine when stopping

- observation of, and safe responses to, other road users

- judgement in selecting a safe and suitable place to stop.

Recap questions

Q1 *When would you not need to signal before moving away?*

Q2 *What are you looking for in a safe place to stop?*

Keep a record

Notes

Your instructor should keep a record of your progress on your *Driver's Record*. You may also like to fill in your progress below and make any notes that might help you, in this space:

1 introduced

2 full instruction

3 prompted

4 seldom prompted

5 independant

References   The Highway Code rules 85,135,137 & 213-226   **Driving** section 5

Safe positioning

Make sure you drive in the correct position for the road on which you're travelling. It's not only important for your safety but also for the safety of other road users

You need to be able to **consistently** do the following **without any help**:

LEVEL 5 Keep a safe position during normal driving

To do this you should be able to...

- use the MSM and PSL routines (see p28)
- follow the principles of lane discipline. Plan ahead and make sure you move into the correct lane in good time
- show an understanding of how a wide or narrow road would affect the position you would choose
- take up the correct position on a one way street
- keep a safe position during normal driving, especially around bends.

LEVEL 5 Respond to the positions of other road users

To do this you must understand...

- how other vehicles, such as lorries and cyclists, need to position themselves
- what clearance you need to leave when passing stationary vehicles or obstructions.

Remember, Plan ahead and make sure you move into the correct lane in good time, don't change lanes at the last minute.

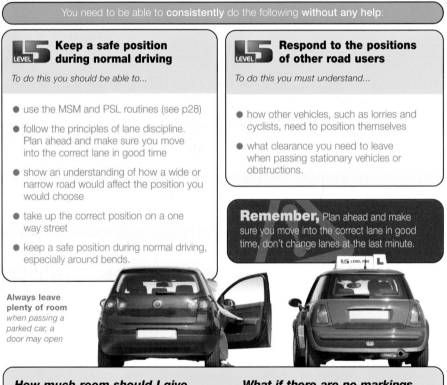

Always leave plenty of room *when passing a parked car, a door may open*

How much room should I give a cyclist when overtaking?

Give them plenty of room, as much room as you would give a car. They may have to move away from the kerb in order to avoid something you can't see.

What if there are no markings on the road?

Position your vehicle sensibly even if there are no road markings. Don't drive too close to the kerb or too close to the centre of the road.

Tips from the experts

Don't obstruct other road users by being in the wrong lane, straddling lanes or weaving in and out.

At roundabouts, make sure you don't cut across the path of other vehicles.

Make sure everyone around you knows where you want to go.

Follow the road markings and get into the correct lane as soon as possible

What to expect on test

Your examiner will watch to make sure that you

- are using the MSM and PSL routines and acting on what you have seen
- respond to signs and road markings by selecting the correct lane in good time
- keep a safe position for the situation.

Recap questions

Q1 *When should you use the right-hand lane of a dual carriageway?*

Q2 *A large vehicle is emerging from a junction on the right, how might this affect your positioning?*

Q3 *Why is it important to move into the correct lane as soon as you can?*

Keep a record   Notes

Your instructor should keep a record of your progress on your *Driver's Record*. You may also like to fill in your progress below and make any notes that might help you, in this space:

| 1 introduced | 3 prompted | 5 |
| 2 full instruction | 4 seldom prompted | independant |

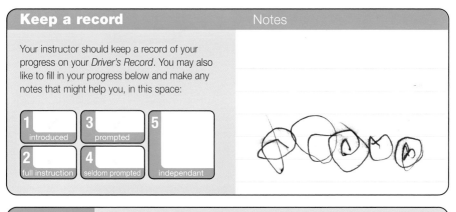

References   The **Highway Code** rules 106-124 & 130-134   **Driving** sections 7 & 8

Mirrors - vision and use

Effective, well-timed, observation should form part of your driving routine. You must know what's happening around you at all times and act safely on what you see

> You need to be able to **consistently** do the following **without any help**:

LEVEL 5 — Effective use of all the mirrors at all times

To do this you must know...

- how to make use of the MSM and PSL routines (see p28)
- when to use the mirrors and how often to use them
- why you need to use the mirrors and the importance of regular updates
- how to act on what you see in your mirrors.

LEVEL 5 — Show knowledge of how the mirrors differ

To do this you need to know...

- the uses for the interior mirror and the two exterior mirrors
- the effect that flat, concave and convex mirrors have on how you interpret what you see in them
- what areas each mirror covers and where the blind spots are.

Remember, there are blind spots between what you can see when looking forward and what you can see in your mirrors. The car's bodywork also creates blind spots which can hide smaller road users. This picture highlights where these areas are.

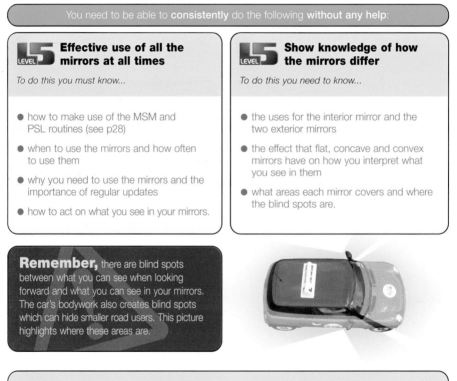

How do I check my blind spots when I'm moving?

It's dangerous to look over your shoulder as you may lose touch with what is happening in front, but you can give a quick sideways glance.

Which mirror should I look in first?

Normally you should look in the interior mirror first followed by both exterior mirrors. You need to check that no one is attempting to move up on either side.

Tips from the experts

Always look before you signal, look and signal before you act and then act sensibly on what you see - just looking isn't enough to keep you safe.

Use all of your mirrors periodically while you drive, especially as you approach any hazard, so that you're constantly aware of what is happening around you.

Never manoeuvre before looking in your mirrors. Make sure that you always use your mirrors before

- moving off
- signalling
- turning left or right
- changing lanes or overtaking
- changing speed or stopping
- opening your car door.

What to expect on test

Your examiner will watch to make sure you're aware of the scene all around, so you need to make sure that you use all your mirrors and act safely on what you see.

Recap question

Q1 *What are the advantages and disadvantages of convex mirrors?*

Keep a record

Notes

Your instructor should keep a record of your progress on your *Driver's Record*. You may also like to fill in your progress below and make any notes that might help you, in this space:

1 introduced	3 prompted	5
2 full instruction	4 seldom prompted	independant

References   **The Highway Code** rule 137   **Driving** section 4

Signals

You need to understand, and respond safely to, signals given by other motorists and give clear, well timed signals to other road users so they know what you're planning to do

You need to be able to **consistently** do the following **without any help**:

LEVEL 5 Give correct signals
To do this you need to know...

- why it is necessary to give signals - you need to signal to let others know what you intend to do

- when and how to give signals (it's important that you time your signal to allow others to respond safely)

- when and how to give arm signals

- when signals are not required.

LEVEL 5 Read others' signals
To do this you need to know...

- the significance of other types of signals including brake, reversing and hazard warning lights

- how to read signals given by traffic controllers such as the police.

School crossing patrols *may control traffic when school children are about. Always be ready for their signal to stop.*

Remember, you should only use signals that are shown in *The Highway Code.*

Should I always signal?

There's no need to signal if there would be no benefit to other road users. If you have a clear view and can see that no one else is around, there's no reason to signal.

Could I signal too early?

It could be confusing to signal too early, for example, if there are several side roads close together. Think about the situation before you give a signal.

1 Fog light

In seriously reduced visibility fog lights can help to make vehicles easier to see

2 Reversing light

Shows a vehicle is about to reverse or reversing. When you're reversing it helps you see what is behind you in the dark

3 Indicator light

Indicators normally show a change of direction, both indicators flashing may mean a vehicle is stopped ahead

4 Rear/brake light

Brake lights can often be an early warning of what's happening further down the road

Tips from the experts

Don't be tempted to flash your headlights for any other reason than that shown in *The Highway Code.*

Always make sure to cancel your signal after you have carried out a manoeuvre. Leaving a signal on can lead to dangerous situations because other road users may take action based on the direction they expect you to take.

What to expect on test

The examiner will expect well timed signals and safe responses to signals from others.

Recap questions

Q1 *When can you flash your headlights?*

Q2 *In what kind of a situation would you not have to signal?*

Keep a record

Notes

Your instructor should keep a record of your progress on your *Driver's Record*. You may also like to fill in your progress below and make any notes that might help you, in this space:

1 introduced

2 full instruction

3 prompted

4 seldom prompted

5 independant

References The Highway Code rules 85-89, 96 & page 71   **Driving** section 5

Anticipation and planning

These skills are found in all the areas of driving. You should always be aware of what is going on around you while planning what you need to do in response

You need to be able to **consistently** do the following **without any help**:

LEVEL 5 — Plan ahead to respond safely to others' actions

To do this you need to be able to...

- use the MSM and PSL routines (see p28)
- identify hazards from clues and respond to them safely
- recognise times, places and conditions which mean there is a higher risk. This includes weather conditions
- use scanning techniques to enable you to plan ahead so that you can prioritise how you will deal with hazards you encounter.

Remember, you'll need to plan ahead to deal with static hazards like traffic lights and road works.

LEVEL 5 — Anticipate the actions of all types of road users

To do this you need to be familiar with the risks associated with each type...

- **cyclists** - take special care when you cross cycle lanes and watch out for cyclists passing on your left
- **motorcyclists** - look for them, especially at junctions and in slow moving traffic
- **pedestrians** - take special care with the very young, the elderly and those with disabilities, they may not have seen you and could step out suddenly
- **animals** - give horse riders as much room as possible and pass them slowly
- **emergency vehicles** - don't panic, check where they're coming from and try to keep out of their way. If necessary pull into the side of the road and stop.

Can I use my hazard warning lights while I am moving?

Yes, you can use them to warn other drivers of a hazard or an obstruction ahead, but only on a motorway or unrestricted dual carriageway (on all other roads you must be stationary).

What do I gain from anticipating and planning?

If you scan ahead you should be able to anticipate potentially hazardous situations. By being prepared, you minimise the element of surprise, leaving you to deal with situations safely in a controlled way.

Tips from the experts

You need to be constantly checking what's going on behind and around you. Planning ahead means that you won't find yourself in a situation where you have to stop suddenly.

Take every opportunity to look for clues like reflections in windows or feet under a van which might tell you what is going to happen next. Even when you're stationary the scene is constantly changing.

What to expect on test

You will be expected to be aware of other road users and road and weather conditions at all times. You will also need to show an awareness of the hazards they present and respond safely in good time.

Recap questions

Q1 *What hazards could you come across on a busy residential street?*

Q2 *Why might a motorcyclist need to swerve suddenly?*

If a cyclist looks over their shoulder, *hold back, they may be about to cross your path*

Keep a record

Notes

Your instructor should keep a record of your progress on your *Driver's Record*. You may also like to fill in your progress below and make any notes that might help you, in this space:

1 introduced	3 prompted	5
2 full instruction	4 seldom prompted	independant

References The Highway Code rules 124, 136-7 & 180-212   **Driving** sections 7 & 10

Use of speed

Your speed should be based on various factors including the condition of the road, weather and traffic, and the presence of pedestrians, but always drive within the speed limit

You need to be able to **consistently** do the following **without any help:**

 Drive at an appropriate speed for the conditions

To do this you need to know...

- national speed limits and restrictions for different types of road and any restricted speed limits for the road you're on

- the appropriate speed for particular road, weather and traffic conditions

- the appropriate speed to use where there are pedestrians and in traffic calmed areas

- stopping distances – know the stopping distance for your vehicle in different conditions and how to calculate a safe separation distance between yourself and the vehicle in front.

Never break the speed limit - *speed cameras are only there to make sure everyone is driving within the speed limits*

Remember, speed limits don't mean that you have to travel at that speed. Use your judgement, drive according to the conditions.

Can I exceed the speed limit to overtake someone?

No, you must always stay within the speed limit. It is illegal, even to break it for a short period of time. Driving faster is dangerous and remember, speed kills.

Can I drive too slowly?

You should drive confidently and at a reasonable speed. If you drive too slowly or hesitate unnecessarily it can be very frustrating for other drivers and can lead to accidents.

Tips from the experts

Don't drive too fast for the road and traffic conditions, make sure that you can stop safely, well within the distance you can see to be clear. Leave extra distance for stopping on wet or slippery roads.

Don't change your speed unpredictably.

Don't approach junctions too fast, or too slowly. Avoid being over-cautious or stopping and waiting when it's safe to go.

What to expect on test

Your examiner will watch how you control your speed throughout the drive and will want to see that you can

- make reasonable progress along the road and respond to changing conditions
- keep up with other traffic but comply with the speed limits
- show confidence together with sound judgement.

Recap questions

Q1 *What's the national speed limit for cars on a dual carriageway?*

Q2 *What separation distance should you leave between you and the vehicle in front on a wet road?*

Keep a record

Notes

Your instructor should keep a record of your progress on your *Driver's Record*. You may also like to fill in your progress below and make any notes that might help you, in this space:

1 introduced

2 full instruction

3 prompted

4 seldom prompted

5 independant

References   The **Highway Code** rules 103-105, & pages 28-29   **Driving** section 7

Other traffic

In most cases, when you're driving, there will be other traffic on the road. You need to be able to deal safely and confidently with meeting, crossing and overtaking them

You need to be able to **consistently** do the following **without any help:**

Safely negotiate situations involving other traffic

To do this you need to be confident dealing with these situations...

- **meeting** - where there are parked cars or obstructions on your side of the road you must be prepared to give way to oncoming traffic. On narrow roads you may need to use passing places

- **crossing** - you normally need to cross the path of other traffic if you're turning right into a side road or driveway. Make sure you position your car correctly, as close to the centre of the road as is safe, watch out for oncoming traffic and stop if necessary. Don't cut the corner or take the turn too widely

- **overtaking** - overtake only if you can do so legally and safely. Check the speed and position of any vehicles behind (they might be planning to overtake you), in front, and coming towards you before you decide to overtake.

Understand the rules for dealing with these situations

To do this you need to be aware of...

- the MSM and PSL routines (see p28)

- why and when to give way - you shouldn't cause another road user to slow down or alter their course when they have priority

- the significance of passing places, warning signs and road markings

- how to deal with obstructions

- the importance of planning and anticipation and acting safely on what you see

- how to drive on all road types - a one-way or two-way road (including a three-lane two-way), a major or minor road, a narrow road or a dual carriageway.

Remember, pedestrians have priority when you're turning into a side road.

If a driver is indicating, can I pull out before they turn?

Always wait until you are sure they are turning before you move out. They may have forgotten to cancel their signal.

Can I flash my lights to give someone the go ahead?

No. *The Highway Code* states that you should only flash your lights to let someone know you are there as a warning.

Tips from the experts

When passing parked cars, watch out for doors opening, pedestrians (especially children) stepping out from between the cars or vehicles pulling out.

When overtaking cyclists or horse riders, slow right down and give them as much room as you would a car.

If you're going to pass an obstruction or overtake, start planning early and well before so that you get a better view of the road ahead.

If there's an obstruction on your side of the road, plan ahead so that you can give way to oncoming traffic

What to expect on test

Your examiner will watch to see how you

- apply the MSM and PSL routines
- respond to road and traffic conditions
- handle the car's controls.

Recap questions

Q1 *Give three examples of where it is against the law to overtake*

Q2 *Which side can you pass traffic on a one-way road?*

Q3 *You see a car coming towards you on a narrow road, there is a passing place just ahead on the other side, what should you do?*

Keep a record

Notes

Your instructor should keep a record of your progress on your *Driver's Record*. You may also like to fill in your progress below and make any notes that might help you, in this space:

1	introduced
2	full instruction
3	prompted
4	seldom prompted
5	independant

References The Highway Code rules 112-121, 124, 129-133, 138-144   **Driving** section 7

Junctions

There are many different types of junction. You need to be able to negotiate any junction on any type of road safely without holding up other traffic unnecessarily

You need to be able to **consistently** do the following **without any help**:

LEVEL 5 — Safely negotiate all types of junctions

To do this you need to confidently deal with these junctions...

- **T-junctions and Y-junctions** - you need to make sure you position yourself so that you get the best view of the road into which you are turning

- **crossroads** - always check who has priority as you approach a crossroads and be aware of the movement of any other traffic

- **sliproads** - these are there to help you match your speed to that of the traffic on the main road

- **unmarked junctions** - be cautious, no one has priority here

- **junctions on all types of roads** - urban and rural roads, dual carriageways and one-way streets.

LEVEL 5 — Understand the rules for dealing with junctions

To do this you need to be aware of the...

- MSM and PSL routines (see p28)

- rules for turning at, entering into and emerging from a junction. These include the need to position your car correctly, adjust your speed and stop if necessary

- significance of advance warning signs and road markings and acting correctly on what you see

- rules of priority, especially when dealing with unmarked junctions

- importance of good observation.

Remember, you need to look both ways, even if you're turning left – there may be another vehicle on your side of the road.

What if a pedestrian is crossing the road into which I am turning?

You should be checking as you appoach the turning. A pedestrian who has already started to cross has priority, so give way. Remember, they might not have seen you.

How can I improve my view of the road into which I'm turning?

Sometimes buildings, hedges, bends in the road or parked cars can obscure your view. Edge forward slowly until you can see the road clearly before you pull out.

Tips from the experts

In a one-way street, move into the correct lane as soon as you can do so safely.

When approaching a junction make sure that you slow down in good time so that you don't have to brake harshly if you need to stop.

Watch out for pedestrians, cyclists and motorcyclists when you're turning, they're not as easy to see as larger vehicles.

Usually when emerging from a junction, if you're turning left, keep well to the left but if you're turning right keep as close to the centre of the road as is safe

What to expect on test

Your examiner will watch carefully to take account of your

- use of the MSM and PSL routines
- position and speed on approach to the junctions
- observation and judgement.

Recap questions

Q1 *When can you wait on the yellow criss-cross lines at a box junction?*

Q2 *Who has priority if there are no road markings at a crossroads?*

Q3 *How should you negotiate a traffic light controlled junction which has an advanced stop line for cyclists?*

Keep a record

Your instructor should keep a record of your progress on your *Driver's Record*. You may also like to fill in your progress below and make any notes that might help you, in this space:

1 introduced

2 full instruction

3 prompted

4 seldom prompted

5 independant

Notes

References   The Highway Code rules 146-159   **Driving** section 8

Roundabouts

To deal with roundabouts safely and confidently you should have a thorough understanding of the rules which apply to approaching and negotiating them

You need to be able to **consistently** do the following **without any help**:

LEVEL 5 **Safely negotiate different types of roundabouts**

To do this you need to be confidently dealing with these junctions...

- **standard roundabouts** - you should know how to approach and negotiate roundabouts even when there are no road markings directing you into particular lanes

- **mini roundabouts** - you will probably need to adjust your speed on approach because there is less room to manoeuvre and less time to signal

- **multiple and satellite roundabouts** - assess the layout of the roundabouts by looking at the signs on approach. Treat each roundabout separately and apply the normal rules

- **traffic light controlled roundabouts** - priorities will often be different to normal roundabouts here.

LEVEL 5 **Understand the rules for dealing with roundabouts**

To do this you need to be aware of...

- how and when to apply the MSM and PSL routines (see p28)

- the importance of effective observation and awareness of the traffic around you

- how to position your car correctly and which lane to use, both as you approach and when you are on the roundabout

- who has priority when you are entering the roundabout

- the procedure for leaving the roundabout.

Remember, look at all the road signs and markings and make sure you get into the correct lane for the direction you want to take in good time.

What if there is a long vehicle at the roundabout?

Stay well back and give them plenty of room, they might need to take a different course as they approach and go around the roundabout.

When should I start indicating to show I'm taking an exit?

You need to turn your left indicator on just after you have passed the exit before the one that you want to take. Remember to cancel it once you have finished turning.

Tips from the experts

Approach the roundabout at the correct speed so that you can assess other traffic using the roundabout. If you need to stop, avoid braking harshly.

Roundabouts are there to help traffic move freely, don't stop unless you need to.

If you're in a queue, don't move forward before checking that the vehicle in front of you is moving, they may be more hesitant than you.

What to expect on test

Your examiner will take account of your ability to deal with roundabouts without undue hesitation. This will include your use of the MSM and PSL routines, your position, speed on approach, observation and judgement throughout.

Recap question

Q1 *Why would a cyclist signal right but stay in the left-hand lane as they approach a roundabout?*

Keep a record

Your instructor should keep a record of your progress on your *Driver's Record*. You may also like to fill in your progress below and make any notes that might help you, in this space:

1 introduced

2 full instruction

3 prompted

4 seldom prompted

5 independant

Notes

References   The Highway Code rules 160-166   **Driving** section 8

Pedestrian crossings

You should be aware of the basic rules which apply to all pedestrian crossings but you also need to know the differences between each type of crossing

You need to be able to **consistently** do the following **without any help**:

LEVEL 5 — Safely negotiate different types of crossings

To do this you need to deal confidently with these types of crossings...

- **crossings controlled by lights** - pelican, puffin and toucan crossings

- **zebra crossings** - which have no lights controlling them

- **school crossing patrols** - these are not always at marked crossings

- **split crossings** - this includes crossings which are staggered and those which have a central refuge.

Remember, it's illegal to park on a crossing or on the zig-zag lines on either side of the crossing. It's also illegal to overtake the vehicle nearest the crossing.

LEVEL 5 — Understand the rules for using crossings

To do this you need to be aware of...

- the importance of effective scanning further down the road

- how to recognise the different types of crossing from their visual characteristics

- how you should apply the MSM and PSL routines (see p28)

- the correct speed at which to approach the crossings and the rules concerning overtaking near crossings

- when you need to stop for pedestrians who are waiting to cross

- the times and places where there is likely to be high risk, for example near schools

- the effect different weather conditions have on your ability to see and stop safely.

Can I wave to let a pedestrian know they can cross?

You should never wave pedestrians across in front of you as you could lead them into danger. Let them decide for themselves when it's safe to cross.

What should I look for when I'm approaching a crossing?

Watch out for pedestrians walking close to crossings, especially zebra crossings, as they may start to cross without looking at the traffic.

Tips from the experts

Make sure you approach all crossings at a speed which allows you to stop safely if you need to.

As you approach a zebra crossing, make sure you are aware of all pedestrians who may be intending to use the crossing.

Be patient when you're waiting at a crossing, don't try to hurry those who are crossing by revving your engine, sounding your horn or edging forward.

If you are waiting in a queue of traffic, don't straddle a crossing. Hold back, the lights may change or someone may want to cross before you are able to move off

What to expect on test

Your examiner will watch carefully to take account of how you deal with pedestrian crossings during your test. This includes how you prepare on the approach to crossings even when you do not have to stop to let pedestrians cross.

Recap questions

Q1 *Which type of crossing has a flashing amber phase, and what does it mean for you as a driver?*

Q2 *What do the zig-zag lines at a crossing mean?*

Keep a record

Your instructor should keep a record of your progress on your *Driver's Record*. You may also like to fill in your progress below and make any notes that might help you, in this space:

1 introduced
2 full instruction
3 prompted
4 seldom prompted
5 independant

Notes

References   The Highway Code rules 167-175   **Driving** section 7

Dual carriageways

Some dual carriageways with slip roads are similar to motorways, you should be confident using these higher speed roads as well as dual carriageways where traffic can cross and turn right

You need to be able to **consistently** do the following **without any help**:

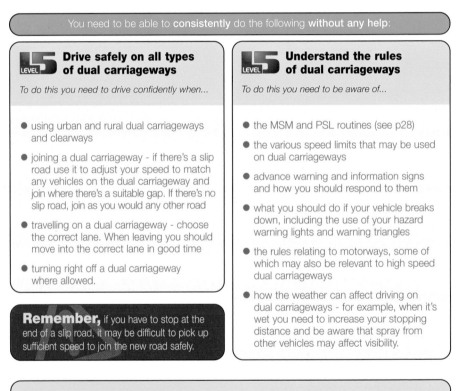

LEVEL 5 Drive safely on all types of dual carriageways

To do this you need to drive confidently when...

- using urban and rural dual carriageways and clearways

- joining a dual carriageway - if there's a slip road use it to adjust your speed to match any vehicles on the dual carriageway and join where there's a suitable gap. If there's no slip road, join as you would any other road

- travelling on a dual carriageway - choose the correct lane. When leaving you should move into the correct lane in good time

- turning right off a dual carriageway where allowed.

Remember, if you have to stop at the end of a slip road, it may be difficult to pick up sufficient speed to join the new road safely.

LEVEL 5 Understand the rules of dual carriageways

To do this you need to be aware of...

- the MSM and PSL routines (see p28)

- the various speed limits that may be used on dual carriageways

- advance warning and information signs and how you should respond to them

- what you should do if your vehicle breaks down, including the use of your hazard warning lights and warning triangles

- the rules relating to motorways, some of which may also be relevant to high speed dual carriageways

- how the weather can affect driving on dual carriageways - for example, when it's wet you need to increase your stopping distance and be aware that spray from other vehicles may affect visibility.

When can I use the right lane?

On some dual carriageways the lane on the right may be used for traffic turning right as well as for overtaking. If you're overtaking, watch for clues that traffic ahead of you is slowing down to turn right.

Can you overtake on the nearside of another vehicle?

You shouldn't normally overtake on the left, but you can if the traffic is moving slowly in queues and the queue in the right-hand lane is moving more slowly.

Tips from the experts

If there's no slip road, join as you would any other road. If you're turning right onto a dual carriageway make sure that the central reservation is deep enough to protect your vehicle. If it isn't, you'll have to wait until the carriageway is clear in both directions before you start to cross.

When travelling on a high speed dual carriageway remember that situations can change very quickly - use your mirrors constantly so that you always know what is happening around you.

If you have to use an emergency phone stand so that you're facing the traffic on your side of the road. You need to be able to see traffic as it approaches

What to expect on test

Where possible your examiner will take you onto a high speed road and watch to make sure that you join the road safely, use your mirrors effectively and drive according to the higher speed of traffic around you.

Recap questions

Q1 *Which lane should you normally drive in when travelling on a dual carriageway?*

Q2 *If you break down on a dual carriageway, how far away from your vehicle should you place a warning triangle?*

Keep a record

Your instructor should keep a record of your progress on your *Driver's Record*. You may also like to fill in your progress below and make any notes that might help you, in this space:

1 introduced

2 full instruction

3 prompted

4 seldom prompted

5 independant

Notes

References   The Highway Code rules 116-117, 149, 248   Essential driving skills section 8

Turning the vehicle around

To turn your vehicle around it's often easiest and safest to use a roundabout or reverse into a side street, however if these options aren't available you may need to do a turn in the road

You need to be able to **consistently** do the following **without any help**:

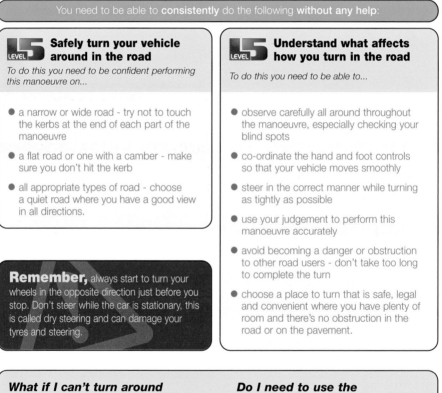

LEVEL 5 Safely turn your vehicle around in the road

To do this you need to be confident performing this manoeuvre on...

- a narrow or wide road - try not to touch the kerbs at the end of each part of the manoeuvre

- a flat road or one with a camber - make sure you don't hit the kerb

- all appropriate types of road - choose a quiet road where you have a good view in all directions.

Remember, always start to turn your wheels in the opposite direction just before you stop. Don't steer while the car is stationary, this is called dry steering and can damage your tyres and steering.

LEVEL 5 Understand what affects how you turn in the road

To do this you need to be able to...

- observe carefully all around throughout the manoeuvre, especially checking your blind spots

- co-ordinate the hand and foot controls so that your vehicle moves smoothly

- steer in the correct manner while turning as tightly as possible

- use your judgement to perform this manoeuvre accurately

- avoid becoming a danger or obstruction to other road users - don't take too long to complete the turn

- choose a place to turn that is safe, legal and convenient where you have plenty of room and there's no obstruction in the road or on the pavement.

What if I can't turn around in three turns?

Depending on the width of the road, how difficult your vehicle is to steer and the length of your vehicle you may need to make more turns.

Do I need to use the parking brake?

You may need to use the parking brake to prevent the car from rolling forward or backward if there is a pronounced camber or slope on the road.

Turn to the right and then briskly to the left just before you stop

Turn to the left and then briskly to the right just before you stop

Straighten up and make sure that you stay on your side of the road

Tips from the experts

Check the road is clear in both directions before you start to move across.

The key is to keep the vehicle moving slowly while steering briskly.

What to expect on test

If you're asked to do this your examiner will indicate a suitable place and ask you to pull up and turn your car around in the road.

Your examiner will be watching to see that you can turn your car around without hitting the kerbs, that you are aware of the situation around you and are considerate to other road users.

Recap question

Q1 *What might you damage on your car if you turn the steering wheel while the car is stationary?*

Keep a record

Notes

Your instructor should keep a record of your progress on your *Driver's Record*. You may also like to fill in your progress below and make any notes that might help you, in this space:

1 introduced

2 full instruction

3 prompted

4 seldom prompted

5 independant

References | The Highway Code rule 176 | **Essential driving skills** section 9

51

Reversing

You should be able to reverse smoothly and safely while under complete control. This includes reversing to the left and right around sweeping curves and sharp corners

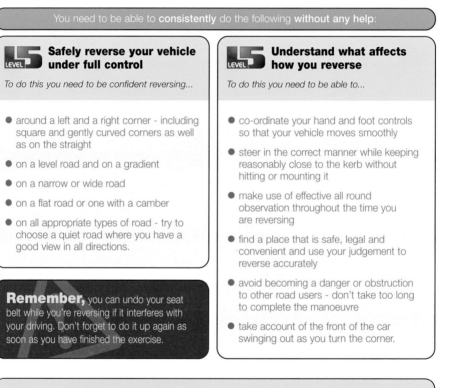

You need to be able to **consistently** do the following **without any help**:

LEVEL 5 — Safely reverse your vehicle under full control

To do this you need to be confident reversing...

- around a left and a right corner - including square and gently curved corners as well as on the straight
- on a level road and on a gradient
- on a narrow or wide road
- on a flat road or one with a camber
- on all appropriate types of road - try to choose a quiet road where you have a good view in all directions.

Remember, you can undo your seat belt while you're reversing if it interferes with your driving. Don't forget to do it up again as soon as you have finished the exercise.

LEVEL 5 — Understand what affects how you reverse

To do this you need to be able to...

- co-ordinate your hand and foot controls so that your vehicle moves smoothly
- steer in the correct manner while keeping reasonably close to the kerb without hitting or mounting it
- make use of effective all round observation throughout the time you are reversing
- find a place that is safe, legal and convenient and use your judgement to reverse accurately
- avoid becoming a danger or obstruction to other road users - don't take too long to complete the manoeuvre
- take account of the front of the car swinging out as you turn the corner.

Where should I look when I'm reversing?

Look mainly out of the back window, but don't forget to check all around throughout the time you're reversing and particularly at the point of turn.

How far should I aim to be from the kerb?

Keep parallel and reasonably close to the kerb all the time you're reversing.

Your car will swing out at the front as you reverse around the corner. Keep a good lookout for traffic and pedestrians in both roads

Tips from the experts

As you reverse, keep a good lookout for traffic and pedestrians, especially in the road into which you are reversing.

Finish by straightening up your car and continue to reverse for a reasonable distance along the road into which you have reversed.

What to expect on test

Your examiner will ask you to pull up just before a side road on your left if they want you to reverse into it.

You may be asked to reverse into a road on your right if your view to the rear is restricted, for example if you are in a van.

Your examiner will watch to make sure you reverse under full control keeping reasonably close to the kerb. They will assess your observation, and responses to other road users.

Recap questions

Q1 *How would other road users know that you intend to reverse?*

Q2 *Into what type of road should you not reverse?*

Keep a record

Your instructor should keep a record of your progress on your *Driver's Record*. You may also like to fill in your progress below and make any notes that might help you, in this space:

1 introduced

2 full instruction

3 prompted

4 seldom prompted

5 independant

Notes

References   The Highway Code rules 176-179   Essential driving skills section 9

Parking

Whether you're parking at the side of the road or using a bay in a car park, you need to gain the skills to do this safely before you drive on your own

You need to be able to **consistently** do the following **without any help**:

 Safely reverse your vehicle into a parked position

To park at the side of the road or in a parking bay you need to be able to...

- co-ordinate your hand and foot controls well so that your car moves smoothly, whether on level ground or a slope

- steer in the correct manner, keeping a reasonable distance from other vehicles

- observe carefully all around throughout the time you are manoeuvring

- use your judgement to perform this manoeuvre accurately, signalling where it is necessary

- avoid becoming a danger or obstruction to other road users - don't take too long to complete the exercise.

 Understand how you should park your vehicle

To do this you need to be aware of...

- the need to check all around for other road users to make sure that you can reverse correctly and safely - don't just rely on your mirrors

- how to steer correctly - always try to steer when your car is moving, don't steer harshly while the car is stationary.

Remember, you need to choose a place to park that is safe, legal and convenient. You can check these in *The Highway Code*.

Starting position - *the position you start from is important – pull up reasonably close to and parallel to the vehicle in front of the parking place, level with or slightly ahead of the parked vehicle*

Intermediate stages - *you should be able to reverse into the space behind the parked vehicle, within the space of about two car lengths, make sure you don't hit the kerb while you are doing this*

Finishing position - *before you finish manoeuvring make sure your car is reasonably close to and parallel with the kerb.*

Look at the layout of the markings and the space available and decide the easiest way to park

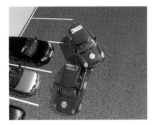

Constantly look all round to check that you're not in danger of hitting pedestrians or other cars

Make sure you straighten your wheels before you finish and you end up squarely parked

Tips from the experts

When parking in a bay there may be times when the layout would make it easier to turn first so that you can back into the parking space.

What to expect on test

You may not have to do this exercise on test, but if you do your examiner will ask you to pull up at the side of the road.

They will explain that you will need to park behind a parked car. Alternatively you could be asked to park in a bay at the beginning or end of your test.

Recap questions

Q1 Give examples of road markings which indicating you mustn't park at any time.

Q2 What's the minimum distance you should park away from a junction?

Keep a record

Notes

Your instructor should keep a record of your progress on your *Driver's Record*. You may also like to fill in your progress below and make any notes that might help you, in this space:

1 introduced

2 full instruction

3 prompted

4 seldom prompted

5 independant

References | The Highway Code rules 213-226 | Essential driving skills section 9

Emergency stop

Effective scanning and reading the road ahead will cut down the risk of having to make an emergency stop. If it's unavoidable, brake as quickly as possible while keeping the car under full control

 Safely stop your car as quickly as possible

To be able to do this while keeping full control you need to know...

- how to co-ordinate the brake and clutch pedals so that the car comes to a halt under full control

- the effect of ABS brakes - you need to know how to tell whether the car you're driving has ABS brakes as this will affect the way you use the brake and clutch

- how different road and weather conditions can affect the way you stop safely

- how to control a skid if one occurs

- how to move away safely again after you've made an emergency stop.

 Look for this symbol on your dashboard, it should light up when you turn on the ignition

Remember, although you need to know how to stop safely in an emergency, it's important that you know how to avoid having to do so by using your hazard perception skills to plan ahead. You should always drive in such a way that you're aware of situations that might develop and have time to respond to them safely.

What should I do if my car starts to skid?

If you don't have ABS brakes, first release the pressure on the brake pedal. If the rear of the car starts to slide sideways, steer gently in the same direction as the skid.

How do I know whether the car I'm driving has ABS?

There will be a warning light on the dashboard and advice will be given in the handbook. Also, ask your instructor to demonstrate how ABS works.

Tips from the experts

React quickly, keep both hands on the wheel and try to stop in a straight line without allowing the car to swing off course.

Know the car you're driving - if the car has ABS brakes, make sure that you've read the handbook and know what to do, as advice can differ between manufacturers.

If you have to do this on test, don't try to anticipate the signal which the examiner will give you.

What to expect on test

You may not have to do this exercise on test, but if you do your examiner will ask you to pull up at the side of the road, explain that you will be asked to make an emergency stop when you are given the signal and explain what the signal will be.

When your examiner gives the signal, try to stop the car as you would in a real emergency. They will check the road behind to make sure it's safe before giving the signal to stop.

Recap questions

Q1 *What happens if the wheels lock?*

Q2 *In what conditions would ABS brakes not work as effectively as they would normally?*

Keep a record

Notes

Your instructor should keep a record of your progress on your *Driver's Record*. You may also like to fill in your progress below and make any notes that might help you, in this space:

1	introduced
2	full instruction
3	prompted
4	seldom prompted
5	independant

References   The Highway Code rules 97-100   Essential driving skills section 5

Darkness

There are many factors that make driving in the dark more hazardous. Judging speed at night can be difficult, so be particularly careful at junctions

You need to be able to **consistently** do the following **without any help**:

LEVEL 5 Drive safely in darkness on all types of roads

To do this you need to be confident on...

- **urban roads** - the variety of different lights can be distracting - vehicle lights, street lights, shop signs

- **rural roads** - the main source of light will be your headlights

- **single and dual carriageways** - there may be a mixture of lighting on these roads.

LEVEL 5 Understand the effects of darkness

To do this you need to be aware of...

- how darkness affects your visibility and therefore your speed and stopping distance especially in bad weather

- when you need to use your lights, which lights to use and the importance of keeping them clean

- the rules concerning the use of your horn at night

- how to park safely and legally when it is dark.

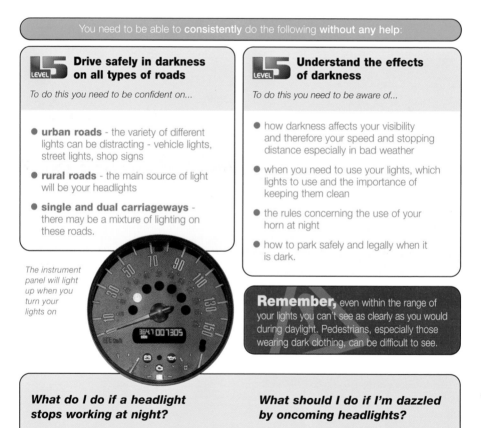

The instrument panel will light up when you turn your lights on

Remember, even within the range of your lights you can't see as clearly as you would during daylight. Pedestrians, especially those wearing dark clothing, can be difficult to see.

What do I do if a headlight stops working at night?

You should fix any lighting fault immediately, both for your own safety and the safety of others. Don't forget to carry spare bulbs with you.

What should I do if I'm dazzled by oncoming headlights?

Try not to look directly at the lights, slow down and stop if necessary. Don't retaliate by leaving your lights on full beam to dazzle the oncoming driver.

You should always use headlights in the dark even when you're driving in built up areas

Tips from the experts

You should always drive so that you can stop safely within the distance you can see to be clear, at night this means within the range of your lights.

Your lights are there to help you to be seen by others as well as to help you see. Make sure you switch your headlights on in good time as it starts to get dark and that you don't switch them off as it gets lighter until you're sure it's safe.

When following or meeting other vehicles, dip your headlights so that they don't dazzle other drivers.

Judging speed and distance at night can be difficult, be particularly careful at junctions.

What to expect on test

If conditions require it your examiner will watch to make sure that you

- use your lights correctly
- drive within the distance you can see to be clear.

Recap questions

Q1 *At night, when can you park on the side of the road without any lights?*

Q2 *When must you not use your horn at night?*

Keep a record

Your instructor should keep a record of your progress on your *Driver's Record*. You may also like to fill in your progress below and make any notes that might help you, in this space:

1 introduced

2 full instruction

3 prompted

4 seldom prompted

5 independant

Notes

References   The Highway Code rules 92-95, 222-224   Essential driving skills section 13

Weather conditions

You need to be aware of the effect some weather conditions such as fog and low sun can have on visibility. Others such as ice, snow and rain can affect the way that your vehicle handles

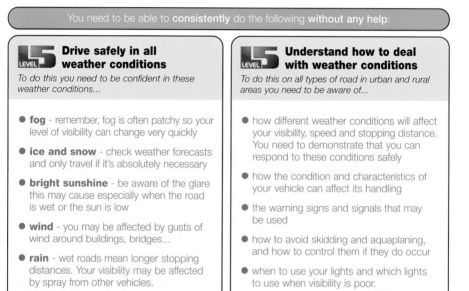

You need to be able to **consistently** do the following **without any help**:

LEVEL 5 Drive safely in all weather conditions

To do this you need to be confident in these weather conditions...

- **fog** - remember, fog is often patchy so your level of visibility can change very quickly

- **ice and snow** - check weather forecasts and only travel if it's absolutely necessary

- **bright sunshine** - be aware of the glare this may cause especially when the road is wet or the sun is low

- **wind** - you may be affected by gusts of wind around buildings, bridges...

- **rain** - wet roads mean longer stopping distances. Your visibility may be affected by spray from other vehicles.

LEVEL 5 Understand how to deal with weather conditions

To do this on all types of road in urban and rural areas you need to be aware of...

- how different weather conditions will affect your visibility, speed and stopping distance. You need to demonstrate that you can respond to these conditions safely

- how the condition and characteristics of your vehicle can affect its handling

- the warning signs and signals that may be used

- how to avoid skidding and aquaplaning, and how to control them if they do occur

- when to use your lights and which lights to use when visibility is poor.

Remember, when the roads are wet, you need to double your stopping distance. In icy conditions you may need ten times the distance.

Be aware that after heavy rain the water in a ford is likely to be much higher

What if it becomes foggy?

Slow right down, it's much more difficult to judge distances and the speed of other vehicles in fog. Use dipped headlights or fog lights when visibility is seriously reduced.

What do I do if the road is flooded?

Stop and assess how deep the water is. If the water's not too deep, drive on slowly. Remember to test your brakes afterwards.

Tips from the experts

Always keep your windscreen, mirrors and windows clean and clear so that you can see as much as possible all around.

You may not be affected by high winds, but be aware that other road users such as cyclists, motorcyclists and drivers of high-sided vehicles are more vulnerable and may be blown into your path.

When visibility is reduced by fog use dipped headlights and, if the distance you can see falls below 100 metres, you can also use front and rear fog lights. If you do use fog lights remember to switch them off when visibility improves.

It's not only bad weather that can cause difficult driving conditions, the glare of the sun, especially when the sun is low in the sky in winter, can make it very difficult to see other road users.

What to expect on test

Your examiner will watch to make sure that you drive according to the weather conditions prevailing during the test.

Recap questions

Q1 *How can you tell that you're aquaplaning, and what should you do to regain control?*

Q2 *Why is it dangerous to leave your rear fog lights on if conditions improve?*

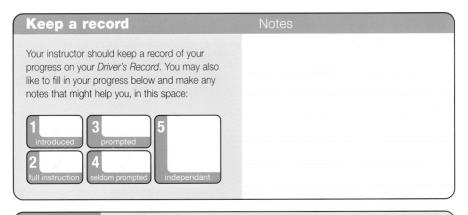

Keep a record

Your instructor should keep a record of your progress on your *Driver's Record*. You may also like to fill in your progress below and make any notes that might help you, in this space:

1 introduced
2 full instruction
3 prompted
4 seldom prompted
5 independant

Notes

References | The Highway Code rules 201-212 | **Essential driving skills** section 12

Environmental issues

Everything from the type of car to its fuel consumption and the way in which you drive influences the environment. You need to understand how to minimise the effects

You need to be able to **consistently** do the following **without any help**:

L5 LEVEL Understand how driving affects the environment

To do this you need to be aware of...

- **air pollution** - the effect that vehicle exhaust gases have on the climate, your health and the health and safety of others. Understand the beneficial effect of catalytic converters on the environment

- **noise pollution** - try to avoid making unnecessary noise, especially when travelling at night or in residential areas.

L5 LEVEL Minimise your effect on the environment

To do this you need to know how you can...

- change your driving style so that you cause less damage to the environment

- maintain your vehicle in a good condition to make it run more efficiently

- dispose of vehicle waste such as spent oil, old batteries and used tyres correctly

- reduce your fuel consumption by limiting your use of air conditioning and removing any unnecessary load

- use the highest possible gear without making the engine struggle.

It's illegal to pour oil down the drain - *you need to dispose of it correctly*

WASTE OIL

Remember, many of the suggestions for reducing environmental impact will also reduce your motoring costs.

Does my speed really affect my fuel consumption?

Yes, it makes a big difference. If you travel at 70 mph you're likely to use up to 30% more fuel than if you covered the same distance at 50 mph.

Does the car I buy make a big difference?

Try to choose a vehicle with low fuel consumption. For further information about fuel and CO_2 emissions, check out **www.vcacarfueldata.org.uk**

Tips from the experts

Use your hazard perception skills to plan ahead so that you can avoid harsh braking and acceleration. Driving smoothly can reduce your fuel consumption by about 15% as well as reducing the wear and tear on your vehicle.

Reverse into a parking space so that you can drive out of it. Manoeuvring when the engine is cold uses lots of fuel. Don't over-rev your engine in low gear.

Check tyre pressures regularly. Incorrect tyre pressure results in a shorter tyre life and may be dangerous. Under-inflated tyres can increase fuel consumption.

Try to avoid using your car for very short journeys, especially when the engine is cold. Also, consider car sharing or using public transport where you can.

Avoid carrying unnecessary weight and remove a roof rack when it's not being used, the drag on a roof box can add up to 15% to fuel consumption

What to expect on test

You will be asked questions which test your understanding of environmental issues during your theory test.

Recap question

Q1 *Why are catalytic converters fitted?*

Keep a record

Your instructor should keep a record of your progress on your *Driver's Record*. You may also like to fill in your progress below and make any notes that might help you, in this space:

1	3	5
introduced	prompted	independant

Notes

References   The Highway Code rules 89-90   Essential driving skills section 17

Passengers and carrying loads

As a driver you need to understand the responsibilties that you have to any passengers, whether they are adults or children, and also how you secure any items that you are transporting

You need to be able to **consistently** do the following **without any help**:

L5 LEVEL Carrying passengers and loads safely

To do this you need to know...

- your responsibility as a driver regarding carrying passengers (other adults, children and babies) and animals in your car safely
- the safest way to carry loads in and on your car
- how to load trailers safely and carry bicycles on your car.

L5 LEVEL Understand the rules of carrying passengers and loads

To do this you must be aware of...

- the rules concerning the use of seatbelts, especially when you are responsible
- the importance of not putting a rear-facing baby seat into a seat which is protected by an airbag
- the importance of checking that all doors are shut properly and that animals are safely restrained in a purpose-made carry box or behind a guard
- how to stow luggage or load it securely and the importance of distributing weight evenly.

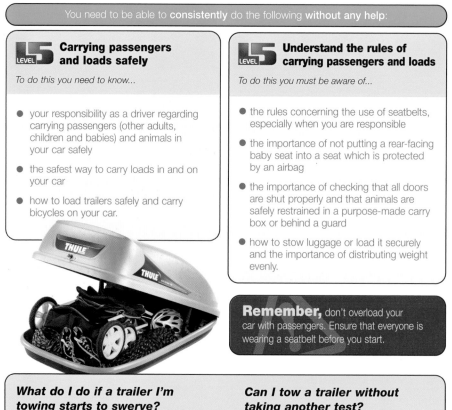

Remember, don't overload your car with passengers. Ensure that everyone is wearing a seatbelt before you start.

What do I do if a trailer I'm towing starts to swerve?

Try to avoid this happening by distributing the weight properly in the trailer. If it does happen ease off the accelerator to reduce speed gently.

Can I tow a trailer without taking another test?

You can tow a small trailer under 750kg maximum authorised mass without having to take another test. You may also be able to tow a larger trailer (see p82-91).

Tips from the experts

Specially designed roof boxes are streamlined so will save fuel as well as securing the load safely.

Special cycle racks fitted on top of or behind the car allow you to carry cycles securely - if they are fitted behind the car make sure that the number plates and lights can still be seen clearly.

If you are carrying a load, make sure it is secure and that it doesn't stick out dangerously.

Any load will have an effect on the handling of your car, changes to the weight and centre of gravity will affect the steering and braking. Allow more stopping distance when you are carrying a heavy load, you may also need to inflate your tyres more and adjust your headlights (see your car's handbook).

What to expect on test

You will be asked questions about passengers and carrying loads during your theory test.

Recap questions

Q1 *Who is responsible for ensuring that children under 14 wear a seat belt?*

Q2 *What's the speed limit for a car towing a trailer travelling on a single carriageway road?*

As the driver
you're responsible for ensuring any baby or young child is wearing an appropriate restraint

Keep a record

Your instructor should keep a record of your progress on your *Driver's Record*. You may also like to fill in your progress below and make any notes that might help you, in this space:

1 introduced

3 prompted

5 independant

Notes

References   The Highway Code rules 75-78   Essential driving skills section 2

Security

This does not only cover the security of your vehicle but also its contents and your personal security. You need to be aware of the ways in which you can reduce the risks

You need to be able to **consistently** do the following **without any help:**

 Understand the importance of personal safety

To do this you need to be aware of...

- the need to stay alert at all times

- the importance of letting someone know where you're going and when you expect to arrive or return

- why you should not leave important or valuable items on display in your car

- the need to choose a sensible place to leave your car, especially at night.

 Understand the importance of vehicle security

To do this you must be aware of...

- how to find a safe place to park

- the different types of security measures available such as steering wheel lock and immobilisers.

Remember, if possible, park your car in an attended or Secure Car Park. For information and to search for secured sites visit **www.securedcarparks.com**

This is one of the measures you can use to improve the security of your vehicle

When should I lock away my valuables?

Criminals could be observing your actions in the car park. Try to lock valuables away before leaving home.

When can I get advice about vehicle security?

Speak to your local crime prevention officer who will advise you on devices and any vehicle watch schemes that may operate in your area.

Tips from the experts

An alarm or immobiliser, a visible security device such as a steering wheel lock or having the registration number etched on all the windows can deter a would-be thief.

Before you leave your car make sure that you remove all valuables (or at least lock them out of sight), close all the windows and then lock the door.

If you have to park on the side of the road at night, leave your car in a well-lit area.

Carry a mobile phone so that you can use it to call for help if you break down, are involved in an accident or feel threatened in any way.

Always lock your car even if it is for a short time, such as when paying for petrol.

What to expect on test

You will be asked questions about vehicle security during your theory test.

Recap question

Q1 *What measures can you take to protect your personal safety when parking at night?*

Keep a record

Notes

Your instructor should keep a record of your progress on your *Driver's Record*. You may also like to fill in your progress below and make any notes that might help you, in this space:

1	**3**	**5**
introduced	prompted	independant

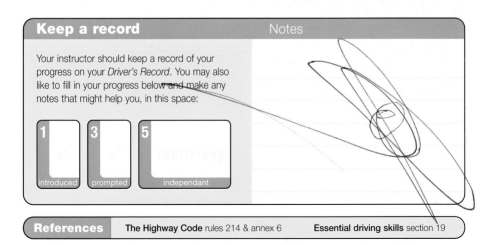

References   The Highway Code rules 214 & annex 6   Essential driving skills section 19

section **three**

THE TEST AND BEYOND

This section covers

- are you ready for your test
- booking your practical driving test
- the day of your test
- the practical test
- your test result
- Pass Plus
- developing your driving skills

Are you ready for your test?

You'll be ready for your practical test when you show that you've reached **Level 5** in all the Key Skills listed on the *Driver's Record*, not before.

Those learner drivers who pass first time do so because they've had plenty of professional instruction and practice. Only 43% of those taking their practical test actually pass, make sure you're one of them.

> **Remember** - your instructor has the knowledge and experience to tell you when you're ready. You'll be ready when you can drive consistently well, with confidence and without assistance or guidance. If you can't do this all the time, you're not ready to take your test.

Are you sure you're ready to drive on your own? - Don't put in for your test too soon, wait until you're ready, it'll save you time and money.

It's important that throughout your training you've been learning the theory and putting this into practice when you drive - you need to do the two things in parallel.

However you do need to take and pass a theory test before you can apply to take your practical driving test.

The theory test

There are two parts to the theory test, the first consisting of multiple choice questions, the second a hazard perception part. Both are taken in the same session.

There are over 150 theory test centres in Great Britain and Northern Ireland. Theory test sessions are available during weekdays, evenings and on Saturdays.

69

You'll usually be able to get an appointment within about two weeks (a bit longer if you have special needs).

You can find out where your local centre is from your instructor, online at www.dsa.gov.uk or by calling 0870 0101 372.

More information about the theory test and the multiple choice questions are given in *The Official Theory Test for Car Drivers* book or CD-Rom.

The Official Guide to Hazard Perception DVD (or the video and workbook package called *Roadsense*) will help you prepare for the hazard perception part of the theory test as well as prepare you for driving on the road.

When you pass your theory test you'll be given a pass certificate. You have to quote the number when you book your practical test and you must take the certificate with you when you take your practical test.

The theory test certificate is valid for two years, if you don't pass your practical test within that time you'll have to take and pass another theory test before you can book your practical test.

It's important that you study, not just to pass the test, but to become a safer driver

When you drive on your practical test, your examiner will expect you to demonstrate what you've learnt for your theory test.

I can't read English very well, so I'm a bit worried about taking my theory test.

You can listen to the test being read out in one of 20 languages, or you can take a translator with you to certain centres. There's also an English language voiceover if you have reading difficulties or dyslexia and you may be allowed extra time in some circumstances - don't forget to enquire about this when you're booking.

How will I know what to do on the hazard perception part of the test?

Once you've done the multiple choice part of the test, and before you start the hazard perception part, you'll be shown a short tutorial video that explains how the test works and gives you a chance to see a sample film clip. This will help you to understand what you're expected to do once the second part of the test starts.

Booking your practical driving test

How to book

You have all the **Level 5** boxes on your *Driver's Record* completed, you've passed your theory test and are ready to take your practical test.

It's easiest to book your test online or by telephone, but you can also book by post.

Online or by telephone - If you book by either of these methods, you'll be given the date and time of your test immediately. You can book online at www.dsa.gov.uk or www.motoring.gov.uk.

To book by telephone, call 0870 0101 372 between 8am and 6pm Monday to Friday. If you're deaf and use a minicom machine, call 0870 0107 372 and if you're a Welsh speaker, call 0870 0100 372.

You'll need to tell them what sort of test you want to book and provide

- your theory test pass certificate number
- your driver number, this is shown on your licence
- your driving school code number (if you have it)
- your credit/debit card details. Please note that the person who books the test must be the card holder.

You may be asked if you can accept a test at short notice, ask your instructor beforehand about this if you would need to use their car. You'll be given a booking number and sent an appointment letter within a few days.

Booking by post - Fill in an application form which you can get from driving test centres or your instructor. Send the form, together with the correct fee, to the address shown on the back of the form. Don't forget to give your preferred date when you book.

You may pay by cheque, postal order or with a credit/debit card. Please don't send cash. You'll receive an appointment letter within 10 days.

Apply well in advance of when you want to take your test. At test centres in Wales, you can take the test in the Welsh language. Please indicate your choice when booking.

You'll receive an appointment letter to take with you when you go for your test. It will include the time and place of your test, the address of the driving test centre and other important information. If you haven't received one after two weeks, call 0870 01 01 372.

Disabilities or special circumstances

Whichever way you book your test, you need to let them know when booking if you have a disability or if there are other special circumstances. However serious your disability is, you will still take the same driving test as every other test candidate, but more time is allowed for the test. This is so that your examiner can talk to you about your disability and any adaptations fitted to your vehicle. For further information, please see the list of useful addresses on p3.

To make sure that enough time is allowed for your test, it would help DSA to know if you

- are deaf or have severe hearing difficulties
- are in any way restricted in your movements
- have any disability which may affect your driving.

If any of these apply to you, please say so when you book your test. If you can't speak English or are deaf, you are allowed to bring an interpreter (who must not be an instructor). The interpreter must be 16 years or over.

How much does the test cost?

Your instructor should be able to tell you or you can find out from www.dsa.gov.uk or by calling 0870 01 01 372.

Can I take my test on at a weekend or in the evening?

At some test centres you can take a test on a Saturday, Sunday or weekday evening. The fees at these times are higher than for one during normal working hours on weekdays. Evening tests are available during the summer months only.

How do I change or cancel my test?

Call the booking office on 0870 0101 372 if you want to change or cancel your test (you might even be able to switch to an earlier date).

Currently you must give at least ten clear working days' notice, not counting the day DSA received your request and the day of the test. If you don't give enough notice you'll lose your fee.

The day of your test

Make sure that you arrive for your test in good time and try to relax. You need to bring the correct documents with you and ensure that the vehicle you'll be driving is suitable to take out on test.

Before your test, you will have to sign a declaration that your insurance is in order and that you meet the residency requirements

Documents

When you arrive at the test centre you need to have with you

- your provisional driving licence - if you have a photocard licence you must bring both parts with you
- your theory test pass certificate
- some photo identification if your licence doesn't show your photograph (see p96). This may change, check before your test.

Don't forget, if you have completed a *Driver's Record*, bring this with you as well.

Any of the following licences are acceptable

- a provisional driving licence issued in Great Britain or Northern Ireland, or a full GB or NI licence giving the provisional entitlement
- an EC/EEA licence accompanied by a GB licence counterpart, if you want to take a test for a category not covered by your full EU licence.

If you have a full driving licence which was issued in another country but isn't eligible for exchange for a GB licence, you must have a GB provisional licence. Your examiner will not be able to conduct the test if you can't produce one of these licences.

All documents must be original - DSA can't accept photocopies.

Your test vehicle

Make sure that the vehicle you're going to drive during the test is

- legally roadworthy and has a current MOT test certificate if it needs one
- mechanically sound and all equipment required by law must be fitted and working correctly, for example the speedometer must show mph and kph. In some cars the spare wheel is a space-saver intended for temporary use only. You can't take your test if one of these is in use

• fully covered by insurance for its present use and for you to drive - your examiner will ask you to sign a declaration that your insurance is in order before you take your test.

A hire car is unlikely to be insured for the driving test. You should check with the hire company when you hire the car.

The vehicle should also have

• a valid tax disc displayed

• L-plates (or, if you wish, D-plates, if taking your test in Wales) displayed to the front and rear of the vehicle - don't fix them to the windscreen or back window as both you and your examiner should have a clear view of the road

• seat belts - make sure they're clean and work properly

• head restraints fitted ('slip-on' type head restraints are not permissible on test).

• an additional interior rear-view mirror for the examiner to use.

Can I take my test in an automatic car?

You can, but if you pass you'll only get a full licence to drive an automatic.

There is sometimes some confusion about what is classed as an automatic, but for driving test purposes only vehicles with three pedals (accelerator, brake and clutch) are classed as manual, vehicles with two pedals are classed as automatics.

The controls, seating, equipment or any other objects in the vehicle must be arranged so that they don't interfere with the conduct of the test. A dual accelerator (if fitted) must be removed before the test.

Remember, if you overlook any of these your test will be cancelled and you'll lose your fee. Make sure your vehice is suitable for the test well in advance.

You won't be able to take your test if your vehicle isn't suitable, for example if it

• has no clear view to the rear - other than by use of the exterior mirrors

• has only a driver's seat

• has more than eight passenger seats or is over 3.5 tonnes in weight

• doesn't have seat belts or head restraints fitted to the front passenger seat

• has been subject to a manufacturer's recall but you don't have a certificate showing that the work has been carried out

• is loaded or partly loaded

• is towing a trailer (see p82-91).

The practical test

The driving test is straightforward. Try to relax and drive as you've been driving during your lessons and practice. If you've reached **Level 5** in all the Key Skills, you know you can do it.

Your examiner wants you to do well and will try to help you relax. If you want to talk during the test, that won't be a problem - your examiner will talk with you but might not say too much because they don't want to distract you from your driving. Don't worry if you make a mistake, keep calm and concentrate on your driving for the rest of the test. Unless it is a serious or dangerous fault you won't fail on this unless you make the same mistake a number of times.

You'll pass if you can show your examiner that you can drive safely and demonstrate, through your driving, that you have a thorough knowledge of the rules of *The Highway Code* and the theory of driving safely.

Throughout the test your examiner will be watching how you drive and how you put into practice everything you've learnt for your theory test.

Does the standard of the test vary?

No, all examiners are trained to assess tests to the same standard. The test routes are designed to include a range of typical road and traffic conditions and the examiners are closely supervised to make sure they follow the national standard. A senior examiner sits in on some tests to make sure the examiner is assessing the standard of your driving properly. If this happens on your test, don't worry they won't be looking at you, so just carry on as if they weren't there.

Can anyone accompany me on the test?

Yes, your instructor or a friend can be present during your test, but they must not take any part in it. It can be beneficial for you to have your instructor sitting in because then they can discuss your test with you later.

If you need an interpreter you can bring one with you, but they mustn't be an Approved Driving Instructor. Anyone accompanying you must be 16 or over and wear a seat belt.

You must satisfy them that you have fully understood all aspects especially

- alertness and concentration
- courtesy and consideration
- care in the use of the controls to reduce mechanical wear and tear
- awareness of stopping distances, speed limits and safety margins in all conditions
- hazard awareness
- correct action concerning pedestrians and other vulnerable road users
- dealing with other types of vehicle in the correct manner
- road and traffic signs.

The test lasts for about 40 minutes. The route has been selected to include as many different road and traffic conditions as possible.

Your examiner will give you directions clearly and in good time, but if you're not sure about anything, just ask. Your examiner understands that you might be nervous and won't mind explaining again.

Apart from general driving, your test will include...

Eyesight test - before you get into your car your examiner will point out a vehicle at a suitable distance and ask you to read its number plate. You must satisfy them that you can read it as detailed on p8. If you need glasses or contact lenses to read the number plate, that's fine, but you must wear them during the test and whenever you drive.

If you can't speak English or have difficulty reading, you may copy down what you see.

If your answer is incorrect, your examiner will measure the exact distance and repeat the test. If you fail the eyesight test, your test will go no further.

Safety checks - your examiner will ask you two questions about carrying out safety checks on your vehicle before the start of your test (see p24)

Special exercises - you'll be asked to carry out two of the following exercises during your test. These will take place at carefully selected places - your examiner will ask you to pull up, explain the exercise and ask you to carry it out:
- reversing round a corner
- turning in the road
- reverse parking (either in a bay at the test centre or on the side of the road)

Emergency stop - you may be asked to carry out an emergency stop.

How the examiner records faults

Total   S   D

① ② ③④

Total Faults □ ⑤

① **Driving fault -** a less serious fault, but an accumulation of these may result in failure

② **Area total -** the number of driving faults made in one area

③ **Serious fault -** committing one of these will result in failure

④ **Dangerous fault -** committing one of these will result in failure

⑤ **Overall total -** the total number of driving faults made in all areas during the test

How your driving test is assessed

Your examiner will assess any errors you make and, depending on how serious they are, record them on the Driving Test Report form. You'll fail your test if you commit a serious or dangerous fault. You'll also fail if you commit more than 15 driving faults.

The examiner will use the following criteria:

Driving fault - less serious, but has been assessed as such because of circumstances at that particular time. An accumulation of more than 15 driving faults will result in failure.

Serious fault - recorded when a potentially dangerous incident has occurred or a habitual driving fault indicates a serious weakness in a candidate's driving.

Dangerous fault - recorded when a fault is assessed as having caused actual danger during the test.

Guidance after the test

At the end of the test you'll be offered some general guidance to explain your Driving Test Report.

The Data Protection Act prevents your instructor from talking to your examiner about your practical test without your permission. If your instructor is already in the car, your examiner will ask if you're happy for them to remain in the car while you hear the result of the test.

If they're not in the car and you would like them to hear the result or be there to listen to the debrief, tell the examiner that you would like them to be present. If you didn't pass your test this can help your instructor to plan any further training you might need.

Your test result

If you don't pass

Your driving isn't up to the standard required. You made mistakes which could have caused danger on the road.

Your examiner will help you by

- giving you a Driving Test Report form. This will show all the faults marked during the test and includes notes to explain the report
- explaining briefly why you haven't passed.

Listen to your examiner carefully. They will be able to help you by pointing out the aspects of your driving which you need to improve.

Study the Driving Test Report. It will include notes to help you understand how the examiner marks the form. You may then find it helpful to refer to the relevant sections in this book.

Show your copy of the report to your instructor, who will advise and help you to correct the faults. Listen to your instructor's advice carefully and get as much practice as you can. You can't take another test for at least 10 days.

Right of appeal - You'll obviously be disappointed if you don't pass your driving test. Although your examiner's decision can't be changed, if you think your test wasn't carried out according to the regulations, you have the right to appeal.

If you live in England and Wales you have six months after the issue of the Statement of Failure in which to appeal (Magistrates' Courts Act 1952 Ch. 55 part VII, Sect. 104).

If you live in Scotland you have 21 days in which to appeal (Sheriff Court, Scotland Act of Sederunt (Statutory Appeals) 1981).

If you pass

Well done! You've shown that you can drive safely and confidently. Your examiner will give you a copy of the Driving Test Report which will show any driving faults which have been marked during the test and some notes to explain this report.

Your examiner will then ask for your provisional licence so that an upgraded licence can automatically be sent to you through the post.

They will take your provisional licence and, once the details have been taken, will shred it. You will be given a pass certificate as proof of success, until you receive your new licence.

If you don't want to surrender your licence you don't have to, and there will be certain circumstances when this isn't possible, if you have

- a licence issued before 1 March 2004
- a D441 or a foreign licence (CLH or NI)
- changed your name.

In these cases you'll have to send your provisional licence together with your pass certificate and the appropriate fee to DVLA, and they'll send you your full licence. You have to do this within two years or you'll have to take your test again.

Look at the test report carefully and discuss it with your instructor. It includes notes to help you understand how the examiner marks the form.

Remember, special rules under the New Drivers Act apply for the first two years after you have passed your test.

You may then find it helpful to refer to the relevant sections in this book to help you overcome those weaknesses noted during your test.

New Drivers Act

Your licence will be revoked if you receive six or more penalty points as a result of offences you commit within two years of passing your test. This includes any offences you may have committed before passing your test.

If you get six penalty points, you'll have your licence revoked and you must then reapply for a provisional licence. You'll then have to drive as a learner until you pass the theory and practical driving test again.

This applies even if you pay by fixed penalty.

Pass Plus

Pass Plus is a training scheme for new drivers. Its aim is to improve your driving skills and make you a safer driver. It can also lead to insurance discounts.

The scheme has been designed by the Driving Standards Agency (DSA), with the help of the motor insurance and driving instruction industries, to develop your skills and knowledge in areas where you may have limited experience.

As an indicator of its effectiveness, a recent survey of practical test candidates (carried out by ORC International for DSA) showed that of those who had taken *Pass Plus*:

- 93% felt more confident on the road
- 89% considered that their driving skills had improved

This was as a result of taking the course.

Three ways to find out more

1 telephone **0115 901 2633**

2 email **passplus@dsa.gsi.gov.uk**

3 internet **www.passplus.org.uk**

---

* Subject to status. Candidates are advised to check available discounts with participating insurance companies - a full list can be found online at www.passplus.org.uk or phone 0115 901 2633.

What are the benefits?

Pass Plus will benefit you by

- enabling you to gain quality driving experience safely
- helping you become a more skilful driver
- teaching you how to develop a positive driving style which is both enjoyable and safe
- reducing your risk of being involved in a road crash
- saving you money on your car insurance premiums.*

Pass Plus consists of a minimum of six hours' training and the emphasis is on developing your practical driving skills. There is no test at the end. Instead, you'll be assessed throughout: you must cover all the modules to complete the training.

Enjoy the course!

Saving money on your car insurance should bring a smile to your face.

Developing your driving skills

Motorway driving

It's important that you understand the rules and regulations of the motorway. However, as a learner you won't have been able to put the theory into practice, and driving on the motorway for the first time can be a daunting experience. Your instructor will be able to help you gain some experience before you drive on your own. This will help you to gain the confidence you will need to drive on a busy motorway.

If you take *Pass Plus*, one of the modules relates solely to motorway driving. Ask your instructor for lessons in *Pass Plus* or motorway driving.

Further training

When you have successfully completed *Pass Plus* you will have demonstrated that you

- have developed your existing skills
- have acquired new skills and knowledge
- know how to anticipate, plan for and deal with hazards safely
- understand how you can reduce the risk of having a road accident
- can maintain a courteous and considerate attitude to other road users.

Do you feel ready for the next level? If so contact one of the organisations below.

DSA have approved and monitor advanced driving tests offered by

The Institute of Advanced Motorists
Telephone 020 8996 9600
www.iam.org.uk

DIAmond Advanced Motorists
Telephone 020 8660 3333
www.DIAmondam.com

RoSPA Advanced Drivers' Association
Telephone 0121 248 2099
www.rospa.co.uk

RAC Advanced Driving Course
Telephone 08457 276276
www.rac.co.uk/drivertraining

OTHER TESTS

This section covers

- towing a trailer
- retest for those who have lost their licence

Towing a trailer

You must have a full car* driving licence before you can tow any trailer or caravan. The key factors that determine what licence you need are the maximum authorised mass (MAM)** of the car and trailer.

If you passed your test before 1 January 1997 you can drive a car towing a trailer or caravan.

If you passed your test after 1 January 1997

- you can tow a trailer less than 750 kg behind a car without taking a further test
- if you wish to tow a trailer larger than 750 kg you will normally have to take a further test (category B + E) - refer to DVLA factsheet 'Towing Trailers in Great Britain' which is available free of charge. Call 01792 792 792 and quote INF30, or download direct from www.dvla.gov.uk.

Further information

Detailed information and advice about towing trailers can be found in *Driving - the essential skills* which can be purchased from good bookshops or by calling 0870 241 4523.

Useful information on towing can also be found on the following websites

- www.ntta.co.uk (The National Trailer and Towing Association Ltd)
- www.caravanclub.co.uk
- www.campingandcaravanclub.co.uk

* A car includes any four-wheeled vehicle with a MAM of less than 3.5 tonnes which has not more than eight passenger seats.

** The MAM is the permissible maximum weight, also known as the gross vehicle weight.

What if I don't fully load the trailer, can I tow a bigger one?

No, the size of trailer you can tow is dependent on the MAM not the actual weight when loaded.

Do I have to take a theory test?

No, you have already passed your theory test when you took your car test.

A useful booklet called *What you need to know about driving licences* (D100) is available from post offices. It contains comprehensive information about what licence you need to drive or tow any vehicle or trailer.

Key skills

You should consistently drive to the level detailed on p20-67, that is to at least Level 5 in the *Driver's Record*, the standard required to pass a car test. There are however some differences as follows

Safety checks (p24)

You also need to know how to carry out checks on the condition of the trailer body, check that any doors are secure and know how to load and secure a load to the trailer. At the beginning of the test the examiner will ask you to explain or demonstrate five separate safety checks.

Mirrors (p32)

You should know how to use additional mirrors and take relevant observation to compensate for the restricted view caused by large trailers and caravans.

Other traffic (p40)

You should always show consideration for other road users by pulling up safely, when necessary, to allow others to pass and avoid the build up of queues of traffic behind you.

Turning the vehicle around (p50)

The 'turn in the road' exercise isn't relevant to towing, but you need to know how to turn so you can travel in the opposite direction, for example using a roundabout or side roads.

Reversing (p52)

There will be a different exercise normally carried out at the beginning of the test. You will need to be able to reverse the car and trailer on a predetermined course to enter a restricted opening and then stop so that the extreme rear of the trailer is within a clearly defined area.

Parking (p54)

During the test you won't be asked to carry out a reverse parking exercise while out on the road.

Emergency stop (p56)

There is no emergency stop for the B+E test, but you will have to carry out a braking exercise at the beginning of the test (see p87).

Uncoupling and recoupling

You will also need to be able to uncouple and recouple your car and trailer, this is normally carried out at the end of the test (see p90).

Practising

When you practise you must

- display L-plates to the front of the car and the rear of the trailer, these must be clearly visible. You may use D-plates in Wales if you wish.
- you must be accompanied by a person who is at least 21 years old and holds a full EC/EEA driving licence for category B + E (they must have held this for the last three years).

You should also practise reversing and uncoupling / recoupling your car and trailer. You will be asked to do both these exercises as part of your test.

You should practise in all sorts of traffic conditions and on as many different roads as you can.

Practise turning left and right, taking into consideration the extra length of the unit. Be aware of your trailer, especially when taking sharp turns.

Booking and taking your test

Book your test as you would a car test (see p71). However, be sure to make it clear that you want to take a B+E test.

The test can only take place at test centres for drivers of lorries and buses, where there is a manoeuvring area (ask your trainer, call 0870 0101372 or visit ww.dsa.gov.uk to find out where these are). Also, as the test is longer there is a higher fee.

Documents

Make sure that you have your full valid car licence with you. Only licences issued in Great Britain or Northern Ireland are acceptable. Your examiner might not be able to conduct your test if you can't produce one of these documents.

Remember, if you overlook any of these your test will be cancelled and you will lose your fee.

Your test vehicle

The vehicle you intend to drive during your test should satisfy all the requirements given on p73 for those taking a car test. The L plates need to be displayed to the front of your car and the rear of your trailer.

Your test

Your test will include the following parts

Eyesight check - Before you get into your car your examiner will point out a vehicle at a suitable distance and ask you to read its number plate. You must satisfy them that you can read the number plate as detailed on p8. If you need glasses or contact lenses to read the number plate, that's fine, but you must wear them during the test and whenever you drive.

If you can't speak English or have difficulty reading, you may copy down what you see.

If your answer is incorrect, your examiner will measure the exact distance and repeat the test. If you fail the eyesight test, your test will go no further.

Safety check questions - the examiner will ask you to explain or demonstrate five separate safety checks.

Are there any minimum requirements for the trailer I'll be using during the test?

The unladen trailer must have a MAM of at least 1 tonne and the car and trailer together must be capable of 100 kph (62.5 mph). If the car is registered after 1 October 2003, the trailer must have a closed box body.

Is it possible for me to take my trailer test using an automatic car?

Yes, if you already hold a full licence to drive a manual car and are successful you will receive a full B+E licence.

Extendable towing mirrors enable you to see what's behind you, rather than just seeing the side of the trailer or caravan

Braking exercise - for safety reasons this will take place on a special manoeuvring area.

- Your examiner will point out two marker cones approximately 61 metres (200 feet) ahead
- You will be asked to build up speed so that you're travelling about 20 mph as you reach the cones
- When the front of your car passes between the two markers, apply the brakes.

You should stop your car and trailer as quickly and as safely as possible, keeping full control and stopping in a straight line.

Don't drive too slowly or brake before you reach the marker points.

The drive - this will be approximately one hour long. It will include a wide variety of roads and traffic conditions including roads carrying two-way traffic, dual carriageways and, where possible, one-way systems and motorways.

Your examiner will expect you to drive at least to Level 5 standard and demonstrate all the key skills required in the car test. However during the drive you won't be asked to

- do an emergency stop exercise on the road
- reverse around a corner
- reverse park
- turn in the road.

Make sure that you negotiate all hazards and junctions safely by using good, all-round observation.

Reversing exercise - this may take place at the beginning or end of the test. For full details of the reversing exercise see p88.

Uncoupling and recoupling exercise (see p90).

The reversing exercise

The reversing exercise for this test will usually take place before you leave the test centre and you will have to demonstrate that you can manoeuvre your car and trailer in a restricted space and stop at a specified point

To carry out this part of the test you should be able to reverse your car and trailer in a restricted space.

Your examiner will ask you to drive forward before you begin to reverse

You should be able to do this inside a clearly defined area

- under control and in reasonable time
- with good observation
- with reasonable accuracy.

Your examiner will show you a diagram of the manoeuvring area and explain what is required. The size of the reversing area will be set out according to the size of your car and trailer together as a unit

- cones A and A1 are positioned so they are one metre (just over three feet) into the area from the boundary line.
- distance A to A1 is one-and-a-half times the width of the widest part of the unit.
- A to B is twice the length of the car and trailer.
- the overall length of the manoeuvring area will be five times the length of the car and trailer.
- the width of the bay will be one-and-a-half times the widest part of the unit.
- the length of the bay will be based on the overall length of the car and trailer as a unit but can be varied at the discretion of your examiner. This will be within the range of plus one metre or minus two metres but the precise length of the bay won't be disclosed before the start of the exercise.

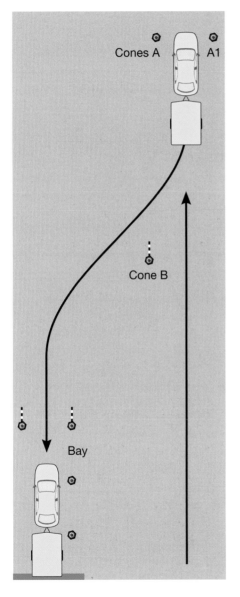

Cones A   A1

Cone B

Bay

Tips from the experts

Approach cones A and A1 in a straight line and make sure that you stop at the cones, don't go too fast and go past them

Turn the steering wheel the correct way as you start to reverse

Keep in full control, don't let your wheel go over the yellow boundary or allow any part of your car to hit any of the cones or poles

Use good all-round observation throughout the manoeuvre

Make sure you stop so that the rear of your car and trailer is within the yellow box.

What to expect on test

You will be asked to

- drive forward and stop at a fixed point with the extreme front of your car level with, and in between, the cones A and A1

- reverse so that you pass cone B on the offside of your car

- stop so that the extreme rear of your trailer is within the painted yellow box area at the end of the bay.

Uncoupling and recoupling

You will need to be able to uncouple the car and trailer, park the car and then recouple the two safely

When uncoupling you first of all need to find a safe place with firm and level ground in which to carry out the procedure. Then you should

- ensure that the brakes are applied on both the car and the trailer (there are various parking mechanisms fitted to trailers, you should consult your manufacturer's handbook to ensure you operate these safely)
- ensure that the jockey wheel, legs or other device provided for supporting the trailer after uncoupling are lowered correctly. If there is any risk, strong planks or metal load spreaders should be used to distribute the weight
- disconnect the electric line(s) and stow away safely
- remove any fitted stabilising equipment
- remove any safety chain or coupling and move the trailer clear of the car.

When recoupling you should

- ensure the brakes are correctly applied to the trailer
- move the car so that the trailer can be safely and easily coupled to it, and apply the parking brake
- attach the trailer to the car and check that the coupling is secure by using a method appropriate to the car and the trailer
- attach any safety chain or device
- fit any necessary stabilising equipment
- connect the electric line(s)
- ensure that the wheels, legs or other supporting devices are raised and secured safely
- check the operation of the lights and indicators and make sure the correct number plate is fitted
- release the trailer brake, ensuring that the car's parking brake is firmly applied.

What to expect on test

You will normally be asked to uncouple and recouple your car and trailer at the test centre at the end of the test.

Your examiner will ask you to stop where there is safe and level ground and then uncouple your car from the trailer. You will then be asked to park the car alongside the trailer before realigning the car with the trailer and recoupling the two. Your examiner will expect you to make sure that the

- coupling is secure
- lights and indicators are operating
- trailer brake is released.

When uncoupling or recoupling make sure the brake is correctly applied before you start

Tips from the experts

Make sure that you carry out the procedure in the correct sequence, that you can do it confidently and without hesitating.

When uncoupling, make sure you have applied the brakes to both the car and trailer before you start and don't release the trailer coupling without the wheels or legs lowered.

Don't try to move forward until the whole uncoupling procedure has been completed.

When recoupling, make sure that the brakes are applied on the trailer and that you use good, effective all round observation as you reverse.

Don't try to move away without raising the wheels or legs and checking the lights, indicators, safety chain and trailer brake release.

Make sure that the jockey wheel is lowered after uncoupling and then raised and secured safely when recoupling.

91

Retest for those who have lost their licence

If you lose your licence after being convicted of a driving offence, you may have to take a normal length or extended driving test before you can recover your full licence.

The court can impose the following penalties

- an extended driving test on anyone convicted of dangerous driving offences (this is an obligatory penalty)

- an extended driving test on anyone convicted of other offences involving obligatory disqualification
- a normal-length test for other endorsable offences.

If you've been given one of these penalties, you can apply for a provisional licence at the end of the disqualification period.

If your licence has been revoked under the New Drivers Act (see p79) you will also have to apply for a new provisional licence.

The normal rules for provisional licence-holders apply:

- you must be supervised by a person who is at least 21 years old and holds a full driving licence for the category of vehicle being driven (they must have held this for the last three years)
- the car must display L-plates (or, if you wish, D-plates in Wales) to the front and rear.
- you are not allowed to drive on a motorway.

You will have to pass the theory test before you can apply to take your practical driving test again. You should study the training materials before you take the test (see p16).

Once you have passed the theory test you can then apply to take your practical test.

Extended test

An extended test covers a wide variety of roads, usually including dual carriageways. This test is marked and assessed at the same level as a normal L test, but is more demanding due to the longer time devoted to normal driving. Make sure that you're ready.

Remember, the extended test lasts about 70 minutes. This is half an hour longer than the standard practical car test.

You're advised to take suitable instruction from an instructor.

You have to pay a higher fee for this test because of the longer duration.

What to expect on test - In addition to the longer drive detailed above, your test will include all the exercises included in the normal test. You will be asked to carry out two of the following exercises, these will take place at carefully selected places - your examiner will ask you to pull up, explain the exercise and ask you to carry it out.

The exercises are

- reversing round a corner
- turning in the road
- reverse parking (either in a bay at the test centre or on the side of the road)

You will also be asked to carry out an emergency stop during the test.

Your examiner will watch you and, in addition to the normal observations detailed throughout the key skills, will also take account of your ability to concentrate for the duration of the test and your attitude to other road users.

annex one
SERVICE STANDARDS

We judge our performance against the following standards (printed in our Business Plan) which we review each year

- 90% of customers will be satisfied with the overall level of service we provide
- 95% of calls to booking offices will make contact with our automated call-handling system without receiving an engaged tone
- after a call has gone through our automated call-handling system, we will answer 90% of all incoming calls to booking offices in no more than 20 seconds
- the national average waiting time will be no longer than six weeks from January 2005
- we will keep 99.5% of appointments that are in place two days prior to the test appointment
- we will answer 97% of all letters and e-mails within 10 working days
- we will pay 95% of all refunds within 15 days of a valid claim.

Complaints guide

DSA aims to give its customers the best possible service. Please tell us when

- we have done well
- you're not satisfied.

Your comments can help us to improve the service we offer.

For information about DSA service standards, contact DSA Test Enquiries and Booking Centre (see p3).

If you have any questions about how your test was conducted, please contact the local Supervising Examiner, whose address is displayed at your local driving test centre.

If you are dissatisfied with the reply or you wish to comment on other matters, you can write to DSA.

If your concern relates to an ADI you should write to

The Registrar of Approved Driving Instructors
Driving Standards Agency
Stanley House
Talbot Street
Nottingham NG1 5GU

Finally, you can write to

The Chief Executive
Driving Standards Agency
Stanley House
56 Talbot Street
Nottingham NG1 5GU

None of this removes your right to take your complaint to

- your Member of Parliament, who may decide to raise your case personally with the DSA Chief Executive, the Minister, or the Parliamentary Commissioner for Administration (the Ombudsman), (see p3)
- a magistrates' court (in Scotland, to the Sheriff of your area) if you believe that your test wasn't carried out according to the regulations.

Before doing this, you should seek legal advice.

Compensation code

DSA always aims to keep test appointments, but occasionally we have to cancel a test at short notice. We will refund the test fee, or give you your next test free, in the following circumstances

- if we cancel a test
- if you cancel a test and give us at least ten working days' notice (this may change)
- if you keep the test appointment but the test doesn't take place or isn't finished, for a reason that isn't your fault or the fault of the vehicle you are using.

We will also compensate you for the money you lost if we cancelled your test at short notice (unless it was for bad weather).

For example, we will pay

- the cost of hiring a vehicle for the test, including reasonable travelling time to and from the test centre
- any pay or earnings you lost, after tax and so on (usually for half a day).

We *won't* pay the cost of driving lessons which you arrange linked to a particular test appointment, or extra lessons you decide to take while waiting for a rescheduled test.

How to apply - Please write to the DSA Enquiries and Booking Centre and send a receipt showing hire car charges, or an employer's letter which shows what earnings you lost. If possible, please use the standard form (available from every driving test centre or booking office) to make your claim.

These arrangements don't affect your legal rights.

95

annex two
PHOTOGRAPHIC IDENTIFICATION

Forms of photographic identification acceptable at both theory and practical tests are as follows

- your passport, or document of like nature. Your passport doesn't have to be a British one, or current
- *cheque guarantee card or credit card bearing your photograph and signature
- an employer's identity or workplace pass bearing your photograph and name or signature, or both
- Trade Union Card bearing your photograph and signature
- Student Union Card with reference to either the NUS or an education establishment or a course reference number. The card must bear your photo and name or signature, or both
- School Bus Pass bearing the name of the issuing authority and your photograph and signature
- *card issued by a Railway Authority or other authorised body for the purchase of reduced-price railway tickets (e.g. a Young Person's Railcard), bearing the name of the issuing authority and your photo and signature
- *Gun Licence, including a Firearm or Shotgun Certificate, which bears your photograph and signature
- *Proof of Age Card issued by the Portman Group bearing your photograph and signature.

Any form of photographic identification presented must be recognisably you and, unless you can bring associated paperwork like a marriage certificate, must be in the same name as you booked your test. If you don't have any of these you can bring a signed photograph, together with a statement that it's a true likeness of you. Both the statement and the back of the photograph must be signed by the same person. They can be any of the following

- *Approved Driving Instructor, but not a trainee (pink licence) holder
- *DSA-certified motorcycle instructor
- Member of Parliament
- medical practitioner
- *local authority councillor
- teacher (qualified)
- Justice of the Peace
- civil servant (established)
- police officer
- bank official
- minister of religion
- barrister or solicitor
- *Commissioned Officer in Her Majesty's Forces
- *LGV Trainers on the DSA Voluntary Register of LGV Instructors.

*Not valid in Northern Ireland.

annex three
PRIVATE PRACTICE

When you go out driving with a friend or relative we would encourage you to record the type of driving experience that you have gained.

You can use these forms to record what you did by ticking the appropriate boxes. You'll probably tick several for each drive, for example, it may have been light when you started to drive but dark by the time you finished. Take note of the time and mileage when you start so that you can fill in how much time you spent on the road and how many miles you covered.

Fill in the time in hours (0.5h, 2.5h) and the distance in miles (20m, 47m). Don't forget to visit **www.dsa.gov.uk/drivinst/drivers-record/** for further information and to download copies of these forms.

Date	Wet roads	Dry roads	Darkness	Daylight	Dual carriageway	Country	Town and city	Overall time	Distance travelled	Comments

Date	Wet roads	Dry roads	Darkness	Daylight	Dual carriageway	Country	Town and city	**Overall time**	**Distance travelled**	Comments

Date																					
Wet roads																					
Dry roads																					
Darkness																					
Daylight																					
Dual carriageway																					
Country																					
Town and city																					
Overall time																					
Distance travelled																					
Comments																					

Date	Wet roads	Dry roads	Darkness	Daylight	Dual carriageway	Country	Town and city	**Overall time**	**Distance travelled**	Comments

Also from the Driving Standards Agency,
the people who set the tests

HELPING LEARNERS TO PRACTISE
the **official guide**

The only official guide which shows how to help a learner practise the skills needed to pass the practical driving test. Essential advice for anyone helping someone to learn to drive.

Most people fail their driving test because they are not prepared. It has been shown that professional lessons combined with extra practice is the best preparation. This book will help the person sitting in the passenger seat understand what the learner needs to practise and the potential hazards they may encounter.

0 11 552611 0 **£7.99**

DSA®
DRIVING STANDARDS AGENCY
SAFE DRIVING FOR LIFE

5 Easy Ways to Order The DSA Range

 Online
Visit www.tso.co.uk/dsa

 By Telephone
Please call 0870 243 0123

By Fax
Please fax orders to 0870 243 0129

By Post
Please send orders to
Marketing, TSO,
Freepost ANG 4748,
Norwich NR3 1YX
(No stamp required)

TSO Shops
Visit your local TSO Shop

Please quote ref **CQD**